LMS JOURNAL
NUMBER TWENTY-THREE

Contents

ASPECTS OF FREIGHT Part 2 *by Keith Miles*	3
LMS POLICY – NEW AND DISPLACED WORKS ORDERS	12
LMS PHOTOGRAPHIC DAYS Part 3 *by Reg Batten*	13
LMS SIGNALS No. 20 *by L. G. Warburton*	21
LMS HOTEL SERVICES *by Bob Essery*	42
OF ENGINES AND ENGINEMEN *by Keith Miles*	43
LMS TIMES	50
THE KETTERING TO HUNTINGDON LINE *by Stanley C. Jenkins*	51
AN INSIGHT INTO EARLY TRAFFIC CONTROL *by Keith Miles*	65

ISBN 978 1 905184 49 1

This photo of the westbound 10.40 a.m. Sheffield (Midland)–Llandudno cross-country express approaching Beauchief station with its 10-coach load was taken from the steps of the signal box just north of the station, on Saturday, 19th June 1954. Nine of the ten coaches were of LMS origin, mostly Stanier, but the third one was an earlier design, possibly from Period I. Stanier 'Black Five' 4–6–0 No. 44944, based at Millhouses MPD, Sheffield, fitted with a self-cleaning smokebox, was built at Horwich in 1946 (batch 4944-4962) and is seen here in grimy BR post-January 1948 lined black livery.
E. D. BRUTON

Designed by Paul Karau
Printed by Amadeus Press, Cleckheaton
Published by WILD SWAN PUBLICATIONS LTD.
1-3 Hagbourne Road, Didcot, Oxon, OX11 8DP. Tel: 01235 816478

EDITORIAL

Welcome to *LMS Journal* No. 23, which is the twenty-fifth edition to be published to date if we include the unnumbered Preview issue and the 85th LMS Anniversary special issue. It is Wild Swan policy to ensure that we can supply backnumbers, but the time comes when the print order is sold out, so I felt I should advise readers that stocks of some of them are not too plentiful.

Since writing the previous editorial, we have made good progress with the Birmingham project, so much so that we have decided to divide it into three parts. The first part will deal with the Western Division lines and the second and third with the Midland Division, but we hope to launch all three at the Warley National Model Railway Exhibition, which is held at the National Exhibion Centre, Birmingham, on 22nd/23rd November. Mark Norton will be on the LMS Matters stand on Saturday, but unfortunately he can not be with us on Sunday. Graham Warburton will be on hand both days to deal with signalling queries, although as you will see from this issue, we are beginning to see further examples of his research, with an article on the LMS Scottish Committee. I am also pleased to say, as in previous years, my dear friend Don Field will be helping me present the face of *LMS Journal* and *Midland Record*.

In this issue I believe we have a varied mix of articles, with a total of five from Keith Miles and Graham Warburton. I am also pleased to be able to publish further pictures by Reg Batten, and a study of the Kettering to Huntingdon line by Stanley Jenkins. *LMS Journal* No. 24 may also be on sale at the Warley Exhibition so I am looking forward to a busy weekend when I will meet both readers and contributors, whose support is invaluable.

Articles should be sent to LMS Journal, Wild Swan Publications Ltd., 1-3 Hagbourne Road, Didcot, Oxon, OX11 8DP. Please include SAE with all articles and illustrations submitted for return in case of non-acceptance. Authors must have permission to reproduce all photographs, drawings, etc, submitted.

3.0 a.m. (MX) Class "H" Rowsley to Heaton Mersey.

Heaton Mersey Exchange

3.0 a.m. (Suns) Class "J" Rowsley to Buxton

Group "C"
(Birkenhead Chester Mold Jcn. Saltney Jcn. Arpley)

3.10 a.m. (MX) Class "F" Rowsley to Derby (St. Mary's)

Derby (St. Mary's) and exchange.

3.25 a.m. and (Suns) Class "F" Rowsley to Nottingham.

Langley Mill
x Ilkeston
x Long Eaton
x Sandiacre
Beeston D.S.) One
   Exchange) Section
Nottingham)

At Langley Mill
Detach
At Ilkeston (South Jcn)
Detach x

3.30 a.m. (MO) Class "H" Rowsley to Brewery Sds.

Central Division
(Group 1)

3.40 a.m. (Suns) Class "J" Rowsley to Longsight.

Group "E"
(Longsight Exchange)

3.40 a.m. (MX) Class "F" Rowsley to Ancoats

Ancoats   ) One
Ashton Road) Section

3.45 a.m.(MX) 4.55a.m. (MO) Class "J" Rowsley to Buxton.

Group "G"
(Ashbourne Line)
Group "H"
(Buxton proper)

4.0 a.m. Class "E" Rowsley to Washwood Heath.

Must not convey wagons fitted with Grease Axle boxes.

4 Washwood Heath
Back fan fitted
Washwood Heath Exchange.

4.15 a.m.(MX) Class "E" Rowsley to Walton.

4 Halewood Exchange fitted
Halewood Exchange
Walton Exchange

At Halewood.
Detach and attach.

4.30 a.m.(MX) Class "F" Rowsley to Brindle Hth.

x Central Division
   Goods traffic
   Central Division
   (Group 2)

At Phillip's Park
Detach x

4.32 a.m.(MX) Class "F" Rowsley to Kirkby

Pye Bridge
Kirkby
Sutton Junc.
Mansfield

At Pye Bridge Junc.
Detach and attach.

7.5 a.m. Class "J" Rowsley to Chaddesden

Derby (St. Mary's)
Chaddesden exchange
At St. Mary's
Detach.

7.40 a.m. (Suns) Class "J" Rowsley to Cheadle Village Junction.

Group "A" Sectionised
x Liverpool
   Garston

May be made up with Group "B" (Widnes and Runcorn Exchange) next to Engine.

x Through to Garston
(Forms 6.24 a.m.(Mon) Cheadle Village Junc to Garston).

8.45 a.m. Class "J" Rowsley to Edgeley.

Group "D"
(Edgeley Exch.)

9.20 a.m. Class "E" Rowsley to Ancoats.

4 Ancoats fitted
Ancoats (including Ashton Road)

At Ashton Road
Detach.

10.30 a.m. Class "J" Rowsley to Longsight.

Group "E"
(Longsight Exchange)

10.35 a.m. (Suns) Class "J" Rowsley to Buxton.

Group "C"
(Birkenhead, Chester, Mold Junc.,Saltney Junc., Arpley).

Sample extract from 'Classification and Marshalling of Freight Trains', September 1952, regarding trains leaving Rowsley Sidings.

ASPECTS OF FREIGHT
PART TWO by KEITH MILES

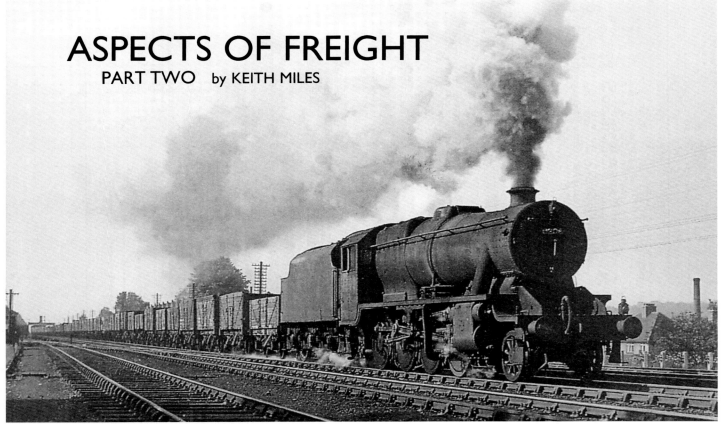

Nottingham's 8206 bringing a train of ex-POW empties, running under an express freight headcode, past King's Langley goods yard in 1947 with the station in the background. The chimney of Home Park Mill, down to the right, is a reminder that it was originally called Home Park Halt at the instigation of the mill owner, John Dickson.   C. R. L. COLES

EXCHANGE sidings were responsible for the ordered dispersal of traffic to destinations within their district, usually by class 9 (BR class K) trip workings, and the assembly of suitably loaded onward trains to terminal points and/or other exchange sidings further down the line. This was undertaken strictly in accordance with the 'Classification and Marshalling of Freight Trains' booklets published for each Division in relation to each issue of the Working Timetable. The accompanying table gives a small sample of Midland Division trains departing from Rowsley in the 15th September 1952 edition, ERO 20735/2, which indicates, incidentally, that there were possibly still grease wagons about three decades after the 1923 RCH revised specification.* The choice of Rowsley as a location was twofold: situated at the foot of the fifteen mile 1 in 90/100 bank up to Peak Forest and a similar climb to Buxton, it was necessary to reduce the train sizes to tackle the ascent. Mineral train loadings from the south were 48 for a class 4F, 70 for an 8F, whereas beyond Rowsley it was 26 for a 4F and 37 for an 8F plus a banker (see my *Rowsley Motive Power Depot*, Foxline, 2002). Otherwise its purpose was to re-marshal trains for onward workings to Manchester and into the Western and Central Divisions.

Most of the Western Division-bound trains went via Buxton, as explained in 'Up the Branch', *Midland Record* No. 12 and a subsequent letter in No. 14. In the same fashion as the London coal traffic tabled in Part 1, Western Division traffic was grouped as under:

A Liverpool and Garston (sectioned)
B Widnes and Runcorn
C Joint line to Birkenhead and Wirral line traffic, Chester, Mold Junction Exchange traffic, WR line traffic via Saltney Junction, Arpley Exchange (all worked as one section into Buxton)
D Edgeley Exchange
E Longsight Exchange (including Wigan Exchange, St.Helens and north traffic)
F Staley & Millbrook (BEA)
G Ashbourne line
H Buxton proper

From the sample listings it will be seen that some trains passed through Buxton, albeit pausing for changes of train crews, while others stopped for detaching/attaching.

Similarly, some Central Division traffic went direct from Rowsley, the 12/2 class H to Walton for instance, but mostly it went via Gowhole, the exchange sidings on the other side of the Pennines. There the onwards traffic was grouped as follows:

1 Gowhole Exchange
2 Ashton Road Exchange
3 Cheadle Heath Exchange
4 Cheadle Exchange Sidings
5 Heaton Mersey CL Exchange
6 Trafford Park CL Exchange
7 Liverpool (Brunswick) CL Exchange
8 Liverpool (Halewood) CL Exchange
9 Liverpool (Walton) Exchange

The Group 1 traffic comprised Central Division destinations: Brewery Sidings, Brindle Heath, Collyhurst Street, Aintree Sorting Sidings and Liverpool Depots. In passing, perhaps I could mention one service that wasn't what it seemed to be: during the day there were three mineral trains entitled Kirkby–Ashton Road. In fact, leaving Kirkby, they comprised

---

* The editor recalls spending spare time at Washwood Heath c1950 looking at wagons; it was not unusual to find some that were registered in the 1890s and many in the early 1900s. Grease axleboxes were not uncommon.

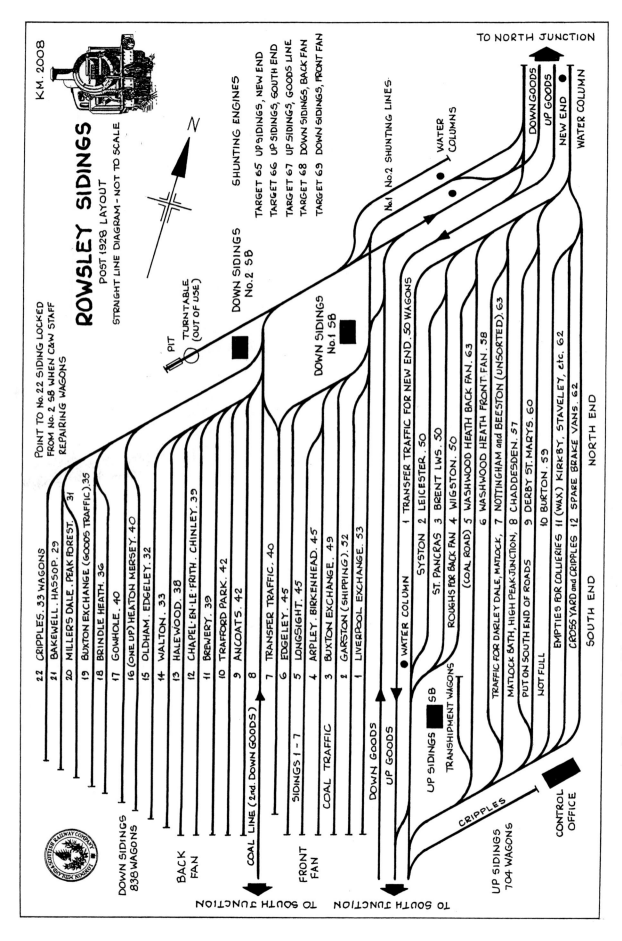

Diagram of Rowsley Sidings giving the allocation and capacity of the various roads.

Gowhole Exchange traffic, and on arrival the engines detached the whole train and attached another complete train for Ashton Road, from whence the traffic was worked forward to the Central Division yard at Philips Park.

Some yards were gravitationally shunted over humps, notably the mechanised yard at Toton, and I've given an outline of operations at Sudbury Sidings in 'Willesden Freight' (*Backtrack*, June 2007). Most, however, were shunted on the flat and M. F. Higson drew from his experience at Burton-on-Trent in his *London Midland Fireman* (Ian Allan, 1972): 'One is constantly receiving and interpreting hand signals from the shunters and just as frequently stopping, starting and reversing. A good shunter will make as few reverses for the driver as possible as he has a complete picture of the work required to be done. Shunting can be likened, somewhat, to a game of draughts with a system for every move and a feeling of achievement on completion of the game. The regular driver soon knows the yard and duties as well as the shunter and teamwork masters the job. It was not uncommon at times of much work for one of the engine crew to help out on the ground, by turning points or coupling and uncoupling, which helped speed up the operation. Much time could be lost when making up fully-fitted trains and extra help was usually very welcome.'

Dennis Hobson, sometime fireman at Hasland, also had this to say in *Hobson's Choice* (OPC 1986): 'On one of my first firing trips, the driver showed me how not to stop an engine when shunting wagons in the sidings. If the engine brake was applied too quickly, the couplings on the wagons could break. So the message was clear; when shunting, before applying the brake, allow the wagons to stretch out and then they would stop as one.' That reminds me of Rowsley driver Sam Stone who had the misfortune of having several breakaways due to rough shunts in the sidings. His oft repeated excuse was that the couplings were as rotten as a pear, referring to the fact that, unlike other fruits, pears rot from the inside, out. The 'Jockos', as they were termed at Rowsley, were the LMS standard 3F 0–6–0Ts which George Bushell found 'a comfortable little engine and fun to drive. With practice one could put the steam brake on, throw the reversing lever over, release the brake and open the regulator. To anybody watching, it would look as if the engine was on a piece of elastic' (*LMS Locos from the Footplate*, Bradford Barton).

Whichever means of shunting was employed, hump or flat, it was the universal practice to allocate each of the siding roads in the yard to a particular traffic. Each road was numbered but some attracted names of their own. At Rowsley, for example, No. 11 in the Up Sidings was known, for some as yet unfathomed reason, as 'Wax', while in the Down Sidings, No. 16, the first road of the third fan, became 'One over'. [When shouted, 7 & 11 could be similar, so the use of a distinctive word for one, 'wax', aided identification. The same applied at Washwood Heath. Editor]

Ken Conquest, nicknamed 'Mr. 100%' after having achieved that mark in an advanced signalling examination of 1952, recalled the road allocations of the period in the December 1999 issue of the Rowsley Association Newsletter and these have been endorsed on the accompanying diagram.

A train having been marshalled, the engine and train crew arrived to work the particular service. The guard came equipped with a watch (provided by the Company since it was decreed that he was in charge of the train), a whistle and hand signal lamp, together with a large bag containing twelve detonators in a case, red and green flags on sticks, a working timetable, General and Sectional Appendices, current Fortnightly Notices, wrong line orders, Rule Book, log book and padlock key. On entering the brake, he was required to check that it was fully equipped with one tail lamp and two side lamps, shovel, brake stick, shunting pole, three sprags, a padlock on the locker and a hand brush. The latter was provided since guards 'were held responsible for keeping the brake clean except at places where special staff is kept for this purpose'. Further, guards 'must see that the screws of the brakes in the vans are cleaned and oiled'. Having satisfied himself on all counts, he would then examine the train to ensure that it was formed in accordance with instructions, all couplings between the vehicles were properly connected, all hand brakes were taken off, all loads and sheets (where provided) were properly secure and report the loading to the driver.

The enginemen, for their part, having previously satisfied themselves that the engine was in 'proper order' and ascertained from 'the notices posted for their guidance if there be anything requiring their special attention on the lines over which they have to work', ensured that they had with them on the engine: the relevant Engine & Enginemen's Diagram, a complete set of lamps, not less than twelve detonators, two red flags, spare gauge glasses, shovel, bucket, hand brush and a set of four spanners. The enginemen were responsible for setting the headlamps in place in accordance with the class of train being worked while the guard placed the tail and side lamps, all 'lighted when necessary'. Side lamps on brake vans, which shone a white light forward and red to the rear, were there to advise the enginemen that their train was complete. Originally they had also been carried on passenger trains but were no longer necessary following the introduction of automatic continuous brakes although they were not finally discontinued until the early 1930s.

As an aside, a couple of the Rowsley Foremen's Assistants acted as guards during WW2 and Bill Chadwick regaled me with one particular experience. He'd already worked up the bank and was returning on a Nottingham-bound service. At Rowsley South Junction no relief was available and Control asked if he'd continue with the train. Bill agreed but pointed out that he didn't sign for the road beyond Chaddesden and would require relief at that point. On went the train, through Chaddesden without stopping and away towards Trent. Approaching Spondon, Bill decided action was necessary and, going out onto the rear verandah, lifted off the tail lamp, hoping to attract someone's attention. It seems that Spondon's 'bobby' noticed that the train had no tail lamp and belled forward 'Train passed without tail lamp', nine consecutive beats. At Borrowash, waiting expectantly on the verandah, Bill suddenly found the brake being bombarded with lumps of coal thrown by the signalman from the steps up to the box. Presumably he'd assumed that the lamp had gone out with the guard perhaps dozing and this was a means of waking him up! 'That's that then', thought Bill, who replaced the tail lamp and retreated into the van until the train reached its destination.

Actually, unless dead tired, goods brake vans were not really conducive to sleep as George Bushell recalled: 'There were

The 12/2 Class H Rowsley–Walton approaching the Millers Dale viaducts headed by 44565 in August 1952. The train comprised traffic for both Halewood and Walton exchange sidings with a stop for detaching/attaching at the former. The engine would work through to Walton but the crew would be relieved at Cheadle Junction. E. R. MORTEN, CTY. J. R. MORTEN

occasions when we had been relieved and had to ride with the guard as no other train was available. Compared to riding in a coach, it was a very noisy trip. Even when the brake was not being used, the wheels seemed to make a harsh grinding sound. The springing was hard, to put it mildly, and at night the only illumination came from the guard's hand lamp or the little coal-fired stove. The intensity of this varied with the train's speed and its effect on the straight iron chimney pipe sticking through the roof.'

All the preliminaries having been completed, the guard, from his van, gave the driver the signal to start by 'holding one arm in a horizontal position', or at night or in fog or falling snow, 'by showing a green light steadily above the head'. This signal was acknowledged from the engine (normally a wave or a toot) and the train got under way. Incidentally, should the train be halted for any cause during its journey, the driver 'must as soon as practicable', after the train has restarted, 'satisfy himself that his fireman has exchanged hand signals with the guard to ensure that he is in his van and the train is complete'.

Now in most cases the wagons would be buffered up as earlier described by George Bushell. On a loose-coupled train, it would be necessary to slowly 'pick up' each wagon in turn since the engine could move up to thirty feet before the guard's van turned a wheel. A vigorous start would, at best, have the guard on his back in the van, at worst, result in a broken coupling. The same sensitive touch was required throughout the journey. George Bushell: 'Although critical about the driving technique of some of the drivers, I always think that those men who handled such long, heavy trains, all with loose couplings and just the engine brake assisted by the guard in his 20 ton van, were real masters of the profession. They really had to know every inch of the way, whether it was a dirty night or thick fog. These trains had to be handled with extreme care, especially after a spell of coasting down a bank with the handbrake screwed on hard to keep the wagons tightly buffered together. 'Picking up' the couplings after coasting, if done too quickly, would cause a snatch that could, and did, sometimes break a coupling hook or link like a carrot. With half a train running loose, there was sometimes a nasty mess to be cleared up.'

I've given several Rowsley drivers' thoughts on the matter in the 'Working the Bank' chapter of my *Rowsley Motive Power Depot* (Foxline, 2002) but here's a comment from another equally testing part of the country. Percy Hobbs of Templecombe: 'The S&D was a very educational piece of road. There were about three places where you could have forty wagons on five different gradients at once. Just a little bit of an incline, level, down and up and down again. A driver had to work his engine all the time: more steam, a little less, so that his back end didn't come in, buffer up, then 'bang!', you'd break away.' ('Templecombe days on the footplate', Somerset & Dorset Railway Trust audiotape *Somerset & Dorset Memories, Volume 7*).

At the other end of the train, the guard's point of view was expressed by Roger Hobson, working out his retirement at the Midland Railway Centre. 'We don't just sit there doing nothing. The guard's in charge of the train and on a loose-coupled freight train the guard controls the train by means of the handbrake all the time. The idea is to keep the couplings taut by use of the handbrake. Well, otherwise, the train could break in half because if you get a snatch and the couplings aren't tight they literally break in two.'

There were places, however, where more severe braking was required: on the steep gradients around Buxton, for example, or on the previously mentioned Merthyr, Tredegar & Abergavenny. These were marked by a prominent AWB (Apply Wagon Brakes) in the Working Timetables and 'Loading of Freight Trains' booklets. The 'General instructions for working down inclines' from the Sectional Appendix are shown in the accompanying panel but, briefly, the guard pinned down the brakes on sufficient wagons to produce a measured descent, the engine and guard's van brakes being reserved for stopping the train should it be necessary. At the foot of the bank the whole procedure was reversed and anything between six to ten minutes was allowed in the WTT for

GENERAL INSTRUCTIONS FOR WORKING DOWN INCLINES.

1.—When it is necessary to apply wagon brakes to assist in controlling a train, the train must be brought to a stand before proceeding on to the heavy gradient or at the point indicated in the following list, and the guard, or guards, must apply sufficient wagon brakes near the engine. The train must then be drawn slowly on to the incline, and the guard, or guards, must continue to apply as many more brakes as may be necessary until the whole of the vehicles are on the heavy gradient. When there are two guards with the train, the guard in charge must apply brakes on one side of the train, and the second guard on the other. When the driver feels that a sufficient number of brakes have been applied, he must give two short sharp whistles to indicate that he is satisfied sufficient brake power is available to properly control the train, and to stop it at any point on the incline, should it be necessary to do so, but the guard in charge will be jointly responsible with the driver for working the train safely down the incline. Should a train be worked by two engines in front, the whistles to indicate that sufficient brake power has been applied must be given by the driver of the leading engine, after exchanging hand signals with the driver of the second engine.

2.—The driver must use steam to draw the whole of the train on to the incline in order to be satisfied that sufficient wagon brakes have been applied, and must not give the two whistles referred to in clause 1 until the whole of the train is on the heavy gradient.

3.—The engine and van brakes must be off when the train is being drawn on to the incline, and be held as reserve brake power for use in emergency.

4.—When the guard has rejoined his brake van he must exhibit a green hand-signal to the driver to indicate that the train can go right away, and the driver must acknowledge the same by a short whistle. The train must not start right away until these signals have been exchanged.

5.—The guard must watch the speed of the train while descending the incline, and, if necessary, assist the driver to keep the train under control.

6.—When a train has to attach wagons from a siding situated on an incline, a sufficient number of wagon brakes must be applied before removing the wagons from the siding, and the guard or shunter must accompany the wagons from the siding to the running line, and apply additional brakes, if necessary, to ensure the wagons being kept under complete control. When the wagons have been attached to the train, the instructions in clauses 1 and 3 must be strictly observed.

7.—The driver must stop his train at the foot of the incline or where it may be necessary, and the guard or guards must release the wagon brakes.

8.—A notice board is provided at each place where **ALL** freight trains must stop for the wagon brakes to be applied.

'General Instructions for Working Down Inclines', from the 1937 Sectional Appendix.

A Lanky intruder, 43612 from Bolton, shunting in a very busy Gowhole Down Sidings in April 1951. Gowhole Goods Junction signal box can be seen in the distance and up on the hillside the tanks supplying the yard's water columns.
E. R. MORTEN
CTY. J. R. MORTEN

Buxton East Junction and 48741 returning to its home station from Rowsley with a 'single' train of coal; that is, a maximum of 26 wagons without a banker. It was entering what was known as 'The Branch', the 1 in 66 curve which connected the Midland and Western Divisions – see Midland Record No. 12.
E. R. MORTEN, CTY. J. R. MORTEN

No. 49387 storming through Higher Buxton with the 4/0 Target 82 Class K to Uttoxeter, Dovefield Sidings, on 28th September 1954. It was at the start of the five-mile climb at a ruling gradient of 1 in 60/62 up to the summit at Briggs Sidings, 1,260ft above sea level. In the reverse direction AWB pertained between Briggs Sidings' starter and the arches on the approach to Buxton No. 2. E. R. MORTEN, CTY. J. R. MORTEN

each occasion of applying or releasing brakes.

Two miles north of Buxton on the Stockport line, Bibbington's Sidings at 1160ft. above sea level was the summit of a 1 in 66 climb and the start of a seven mile 1 in 58/60 descent down to Whaley Bridge with AWB stipulated in both directions. The site has entered into railway folklore following the disastrous runaway of Driver John Axon on 48188 with the 11.5 Buxton–Arpley on 11th February 1957. The initial cause, as recorded in the MOT report, was 'the failure of a joint in the pipe leading to the driver's steam brake valve which not only put the braking system out of action but also filled the cab with scalding steam'. This occurred where the train would otherwise have stopped to pin down the wagon brakes. 'With great bravery and determination the enginemen, after repeated efforts, managed to get the regulator partly closed and to apply the hand brake on the tender, but by this time the front of the train had reached the summit and could not be stopped.' Axon told fireman Ron Scanlon to drop off and try to apply some wagon brakes. Although he managed to drop half a dozen brake handles, the train was travelling too fast for him to pin them down. 'Driver Axon, however, remained at his post to give warning that the train was running away, and in the hope of regaining control on a more favourable gradient.' Regrettably this proved impossible, with a fatal result at Chapel-en-le-Frith.

For the most part, relationships between the enginemen and guard were convivial and they worked as a team. There was, however, a certain disgruntlement among locomen as expressed in a piece of railway doggerel:

> The driver rides on wings of steel,
> The fireman on wings of flame,
> The poor old guard has no wings at all,
> But he gets there just the same!

The point of difference was the watch. Despite the fact that it was the engine and its crew that got the train to where it was supposed to be going, at the time it was supposed to get there, it was the guard who was given the watch and, with it, kept a log of the journey and submitted a journal at the end of his shift. 'They carried a thick record book,' explained George Bushell, 'in which they noted full details of each train they worked together with passing and arrival times. Some had a reputation for having a sharp pencil; in other words they were too accurate with their details! This meant that Control would be breathing down the driver's neck to know why he had lost a few minutes here and there.' Nevertheless, as Alf Lovell remarked, 'Between operating men you had an association, you had loyalty between your mates. The driver knew his engine inside out, he'd keep it going on a song and a prayer, and he knew the guard on the back knew his job. Everyone was as good or as best as he could be on his job.'

Although not exhaustive, these then are some aspects of freight in a bygone age. Out of the public gaze, of course, was the associated traffic control arrangements which I've talked about in 'Improver Assistant in Control', *Journal* No. 17. I'm grateful to those railwaymen, some my workmates, who felt able to record their experiences, both on tape and in print, of a way of life long gone. I can't resist quoting a couple of verses of a song by Dave Goulder, a former fireman at Westhouses, concerning a guard made redundant in the Beeching era:

> So now I know how a wagon feels,
> When the grass comes creeping round its wheels,
> And the timbers rot and the paintwork peels,
> I'm in the sidings now.
>
> I'll give my whistle one more blow,
> Then I'll swap my pole for a garden hoe,
> My boiler fire is burning low,
> I'm in the sidings now.

LMS POLICY
NEW AND DISPLACED WORKS ORDERS

MANY years ago, during a discussion with my dear friend, the late David Jenkinson, he made a profound statement, "You know, Bob, it is far more interesting to know *why* something happened than to merely record what happened." I have never forgotten that conversation and hope the lesson learned will remain one of the themes that make up *LMS Journal* philosophy. At the risk of appearing to be slightly provocative, it seems to me that many authors do little more than repeat what others have said instead of consulting primary material.

The overall *LMS Journal* approach is to record all aspects of the company's policy, and to date a number of articles have been published with that objective in mind. In *LMS Journal* No. 1 we gave the names of the directors and senior managers and the pre-Group companies they came from, in order that we can see who was responsible for forging the constituent and subsidiary companies into a single unified company. The same edition contained an article about the Western Division arrangements for allocating consecutively numbered engines to the same shed.

In *LMS Journal* No. 2 we ran an article describing the introduction of the diesel shunter, and in No. 5 I touched upon the carriage and wagon renewal policy and explained about the engine history cards and why they were introduced. No. 6 included an engine test article, and an analysis of locomotive operating costs appeared in No. 7. These are all part of a theme designed to show the true facts about the performance of both the inherited and new standard engines built by the company.

The years from 1923 to 1947 included some very difficult times for any commercial company and articles in Nos. 6 and 9 underline the commercial pressures the directors had to contend with and reveal some of the changes that were made.

In this issue we will look at New and Displaced Works Orders. For a number of years I have noted the letters NWO or DWO as being 'an authority' for a particular project. I have also noted that often many years separate work that was allocated or authorised by the same number. Unfortunately, I did not know precisely what the letters meant, but finding the paper that was presented at the Chief Mechanical Engineer's Conference in January 1934 answered most of the questions. It has been reproduced exactly as written. For my part, I look forward to reading what those readers, who have an accountancy background, make of it. For the rest of us, we will know that the authority was for either New or Displaced Work and that the allocation of expenditure was made accordingly.

Bob Essery

You are aware of the recent introduction of details of estimated expenditure, which has become necessary in order to investigate the increased efficiency of schemes put forward for approval. Here again it cannot be too well emphasised that it is imperative that the Accountant and the C.M.E. Department should act in close collaboration when compiling the financial results of all proposed schemes.

That co-operation and a mutual endeavour to appreciate each other's difficulties is nowadays essential is nowhere more apparent than in relation to New Works matters.

In the early days following amalgamation the call for financial information in regard to New Works Proposals was relatively negligible compared with what it is today, and the extent and character of the increased requirements in this direction has necessitated the issue by the Directors, Executive and Accountant of a number of Regulations and Instructions which, whilst clear enough in their definition of the principles to be followed, do not, and obviously could not clarify the numerous difficulties which arise in the detailed application of those principles.

There appears to exist in some quarters an erroneous belief that detailed Accounting procedure is "cut and dried", and that so soon as the problems associated with the technical aspect of a New Works proposal have been solved to the satisfaction of those directly concerned, the Accounting staff should be able to complete the matter on the strength of bare statements of what the work will cost, without any of the enquiries which are now so generally made in regard to the "why" and "wherefore" of a scheme.

It requires to be realised that detailed Accounting procedure is no more "cut and dried" than is the procedure adopted in the application of Engineering Science. Both are governed by certain fundamental laws and principles which in themselves are capable of being more or less readily absorbed, but if the problems which arise in the application of those laws and principles to the detailed elements of a scheme are to be satisfactorily solved and subsequent and wasteful revision obviated, all relevant circumstances must be known at the time the problem is being tackled; and it is solely with a desire to understand what work a scheme involves in order to ensure that the expenditure is appropriately allocated and the effect upon the Company's Capital and Revenue Accounts ascertained, that these enquiries are directed.

The lack of indulgence which has at times been manifest at the increasing demand for information in regard to New Works has been found to be due in some cases to an inability to appreciate why so much now requires to be known by the Accountant in regard to the "works" side of a scheme, seeing that such information was never asked for previously, when the Railways made a much better financial shewing than they have of recent years.

Everyone will agree that in whatever branch of Railway activity we may individually be engaged, past history is not a matter of primary concern, except insofar as it enables us to appreciate where progress has been and still can be made.

We are legally bound to charge our fixed assets to Capital Account at their first cost and improvements similarly at their first cost, and to effect all repairs and replacements out of Revenue. We are not legally entitled either to write down the value of these assets in the Capital Account nor to write them out of Capital Account until such time as they are broken up, sold, or abandoned in perpetuity by an order of the Directors, and it is upon the law as applied to Railway Companies that the whole of the allocation procedure and enquiries are based. The very fact that the Railways have not of recent years experienced the degree of prosperity which a number of them enjoyed in earlier years, and that Railway Accounts are being more and more subjected to examination and enquiry by Government Departments and various Tribunals, makes it imperative that every possible care shall be taken to ensure that the Company is not embarrassed in raising new Capital by the erroneous charging to Capital Account of outlay of a replacement character, and that the various Revenue Accounts are neither unduly burdened nor relieved in consequence of incomplete examination of New Works schemes.

It is principally upon the ascertainment of the extent to which a scheme involves additions to our existing Capital assets and to what extent it consists of replacements or work of a maintenance character, that we depend for an estimate of the probable increase or decrease in annual charges which the scheme will occasion, and the necessity for allocation in accordance with the facts of the case will, in this connection, immediately be apparent.

It has recently been said that the submission of estimated costs statements in connection with a proposed scheme can on occasions be detrimental to the Company's interests, inasmuch as a bad financial shewing prohibits the scheme from being submitted for authority, notwithstanding a definite conviction on the part of the Engineering or Operating Departments concerned that it is of real value to the Company, but this is not the case, the fact being that where the "Operating" or "Engineering" justification is of greater import than the financial aspect of a scheme, it will, provided that the relevant facts are stated when application for authority is made, receive the appropriate measure of consideration. Such justification is really financial justification not capable of being stated in terms of $£$. s. d.

Another ruling which still invokes some measure of criticism is that relating to the transfer of Capital assets (principally machinery) from one Department or Depot to another at original cost, especially when it is intended that the machine will only be used in some lesser capacity than that for which it was installed.

As previously stated, we are legally bound to retain our assets in Capital Account at their first cost until they are broken up or sold, and in no case is Capital outlay measured by or adjusted on the basis of productive capacity. However sincere the intention may be to utilise a machine in some reduced capacity (and the sincerity of the proposal is never in question) it cannot be denied that so long as the machine remains intact the possibility survives not only that it may at some future date be re-used in its original capacity, but that in this event it may even be replaced by a new machine at the expense of Revenue, and in such circumstances there can be no justification for writing it out of the Capital Account as having been displaced. Where, under this ruling, retention of a machine for some lesser purpose cannot be financially justified, then for the purpose of authorisation the facts require to be fully stated, in order that due consideration may be given to the special circumstances of the case. Some of you may remember cases in the past where old replaced units were transferred to other places and then renewed, but clearly where that is required it should be done by direct justification and not hidden.

There is neither time nor space to deal in detail on this occasion with other phases of the New Works Regulations and procedure which from time to time have created difficulties and excited controversy, but it is hoped that the above remarks will suffice to shew that there are very substantial reasons for the various instructions which have either emanated from or received the approval of the Directors or the Executive, and that in shouldering the burden of work which compliance involves, we are striving to add to the increasing efficiency with which every phase of the Company's business is today being conducted.

The time factor is all important – but many times the Accountant seems to start at scratch and every job of costing is urgently required. It would be a great advantage to all if, in the earlier stages of enquiries, opportunities were afforded for the detection of financial difficulties rather than spend time after schemes are framed wholly or partly.

You will all find ready and willing help and support from the respective Works Accountants on the system and although the Chief Accountant will not release his grip on the final criticism, it will be a great help to you, because he will undoubtedly say a few kind words to his colleagues when next he meets them.

    (Signed) A. BENTLEY.
                    B. C. OLVER.

National Archives RAIL 418/181

LMS PHOTOGRAPHIC DAYS

PART THREE by REG BATTEN

This selection of photographs was taken either in LMS days or shortly after Nationalisation on the London Midland region. I never took many photographs on the LMS, or the London Midland Region of British Railways, as most of it was to become after 1948. I did visit two places on a regular basis, one location on each of the main line routes out of London. One was at Bourne End, just south of Berkhamsted station in Hertfordshire on the ex-LNWR West Coast Main Line route from Euston. The other site I favoured was just north of Elstree on the Midland main line from St. Pancras, a site I know was popular with other photographers whose work I have seen in magazines. Both these locations were chosen because they would not take too long or be too expensive to reach from my home in East London. Both offered a country background, something I found preferable to industrial or residential backdrops. Both would be very busy at most times with a variety of traffic and motive power.

Each line had its own character. The West Coast Main Line was the glamour line, with Pacifics on the most important trains. From June 1937, the highlight would be the 'Coronation Scot' streamliner – the LMS answer to the LNER's streamlined 'Coronation'. The less important express passenger trains would feature 'Royal Scot', 'Jubilee' or 'Patriot' 4–6–0s as the motive power. The Midland line did not see any Pacifics; the various 4–6–0 types monopolised the long-distance passenger trains. On the WCML, local stopping passenger trains ran to Bletchley, and to Bedford on the Midland line.

In those days there was plenty of freight traffic. The Midland line in particular was the place to see coal trains, working to the London area from the extensive coalfields of the East Midlands to meet the extensive needs of the London metropolis. Coal would be used by industry, for gasworks, for domestic heating and cooking, and, of course, by the railways themselves. The Beyer-Garratts often worked the Toton to Brent coal trains. However, I chose not to photograph these as I regarded them as ugly, and spoilt by the Midland-style features.

I had also looked at some alternative locations, but had ruled them out for various reasons. I tried the south end of Northchurch Tunnel, which is to the north of Berkhamsted on the WCML, but found this unsatisfactory as drivers tended to cut off when entering the tunnel. Tring cutting was turned down for the reason that it was too deep and awkward and the lighting could be bad. At Elstree, I found that standing on the platform end looking south, one could see right through the tunnel itself. You could see the trains coming north, but the angle was too front-on to make a good photograph. Moreover, the view going south was hopeless. But a little further north, there was a footbridge and a road overbridge. This was a fine place to see and photograph trains travelling in both directions. The lighting for photography was best for up trains in the morning and down trains in the afternoon, as indeed was also the case at Bourne End on the West Coast Main Line.

Midland Compound 4–4–0 No. 1013 heading a stopping train at Elstree.

LMS Jubilee No. 5569 Tasmania heading a Midland line express through Elstree.

In early BR days, 'Royal Scot' No. 46142 The York & Lancaster Regiment, still with parallel boiler, is seen here with an express through Elstree. BR numbers had been applied on the smokebox and cab sides, but the tender was still

Another stopping train, another Compound, this time No. 1050 at Elstree.

Maids of all work! 'Black Five' No. 4856, seen here in charge of a train of 6-wheel tank wagons through Elstree.

Stanier 2-cylinder 2–6–4T No. 2539 alongside the coaling stage at Willesden shed. This was taken on a visit to the depot in 1937 organised by the Stephenson Locomotive Society. These engines would be used on the outer suburban stopping trains to Bletchley, the local service to Watford having been electrified on the third rail system.

'Royal Scot' 6145 The Duke of Wellington's Regt. (West Riding), *rebuilt with taper boiler but not yet fitted with smoke deflectors, seen on an up train at Bourne End.*

In original style with parallel boiler, 'Royal Scot' 6125 3rd Carabinier *making easy work of hauling an express train at Bourne End.*

In early BR days, Jubilee No. 45673 Keppel heading an express passenger train at Bourne End, near Berkhamsted. Note the smokebox number plate had LMS-style lettering.

Rebuilt 'Royal Scot' 46139 The Welch Regiment at Bourne End in full early BR livery with 'British Railways' spelled out in full on the tender.

Stanier 8F 2-8-0 No. 8032 on a coal train at Bourne End, near Berkhamsted on the WCML. It wasn't only the Midland line that saw coal trains!

EDITORIAL COMMENT

I would like to take this opportunity to remind readers that it is our policy to encourage the submission of pictures and indeed complete articles. Of particular interest are those written by ex-railwaymen from the steam era that worked over ex-LMS lines. I believe that it is important that we record as much as possible about their first-hand experiences while we are able to do so in order that future generations have a clear idea of how the railways of yesteryear were worked. In this regard I would like to acknowledge the contribution from Derek Ashworth, which appears at page 42 of this edition and to say that in a future *LMS Journal* we will recount his experiences as a signalman at Gowhole, which is also illustrated at pages 8 and 9.

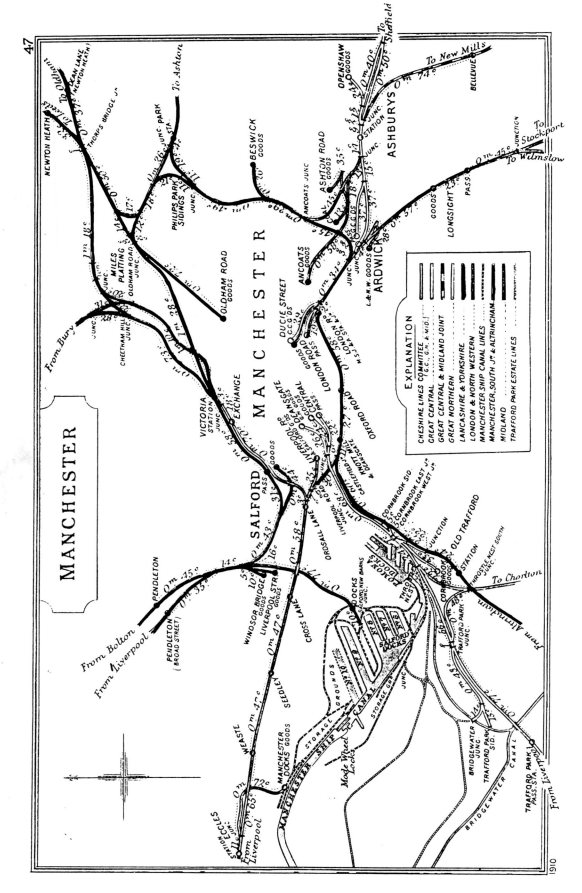

Fig. 1. Diagram of the lines serving Manchester as in the RCH Junction Diagram Book, 1913.

LMS SIGNALS
No. 20 – MANCHESTER VICTORIA AND EXCHANGE MULTIPLE-ASPECT COLOUR LIGHT AND POWER RE-SIGNALLING SCHEME

by L. G. WARBURTON

THE great city of Manchester, once the centre of the cotton industry and noted for locomotive construction and heavy engineering, required an efficient transport system to distribute its products. Apart from being connected to the national canal network, the city was served by several railways. Principal among these was the Lancashire & Yorkshire Railway and the London & North Western Railway, whose Manchester stations were Victoria (L&Y), Exchange and London Road (LNWR). The area served by Victoria & Exchange stations was wide, with a continual stream of business traffic from and to places such as St. Annes, Lytham, Southport, Liverpool and even as far away as the North Wales residential resorts. Nearer to Manchester the stations served Preston, Blackburn, Bolton, etc, together with excursion traffic to Blackpool and Southport. The Midland Railway also served Manchester, terminating in Central station and so too did the Great Central sharing London Road station.

Manchester Victoria Station opened on 1st January 1844, closing the existing stations Liverpool Road and Oldham Road to passenger traffic, and at that time was the largest station in the United Kingdom with a continuous roof 684 feet long. Victoria was extended several times and, when further accommodation was required for LNWR traffic, Manchester Exchange was opened in 1884 with covered foot accommodation being provided for passengers requiring to use the L&Y Victoria Station. The LNWR portion of Victoria was then used for fish traffic and stabling of coaching stock.

The L&Y and LNWR had merged on 1st January 1922, anticipating the grouping by one year when no doubt the idea of more efficient and flexible use of their two adjacent stations would have been considered. The ability to gain access to either station by either company's trains would have surely been high on the new company's list of priorities. At this time there was only one through road in either direction mainly used for goods traffic or long-distance trains passing from one system to the other without stopping.

With the formation of the London Midland & Scottish Railway, the stage was set to prepare a scheme and put the work in hand.

The Traffic Committee met on 29th November 1923 and Minute 246 stated 'that considerable difficulty was experienced in dealing with heavy traffic which

Plate 1. *Exterior of Manchester Victoria ex-L&Y station.*

Plate 2. *Exterior of Manchester Exchange ex-LNWR station.*

PERSONNEL

Much credit must go to the signal and electrical engineers involved in designing this scheme at a time when established signal practice was constantly being challenged, and, as can be seen, much innovation went into this installation. With the LMS Signal and Telegraph Department still to be formed, signalling was the responsibility of the Civil Engineer whilst telegraphs came under the Electrical Engineer, as at this time the LMS had an Electrical Department. It follows therefore that full co-operation was required between signal and electrical engineers with doubtless areas of disagreement.

The signalling layout was designed by R. G. Berry, Signal Assistant to Mr. E. H. Townsend, the Divisional Civil Engineer at Manchester. Berry was previously the ex-LYR signal engineer. V. H. Openshaw was Berry's assistant, together with W. Barnes and several others. The electrical side of the work was designed by H. W. Moore, the Manchester Divisional Assistant to Mr. J. Sayers, the Telegraph Superintendent, also J. Howarth, Principal Assistant. The Westinghouse resident engineer was Frederick J. Flint.

Plate 3. *Richard Golding Berry commenced work as a draughtsman on the LYR in 1890 in the Civil Engineer's Office, moving to the Signal Department in 1891. On the retirement of H. Raynor-Wilson, he became Assistant Signal Engineer under Cyril Beuziville Byles and L&Y Signal Superintendent when Byles emigrated to Australia in 1911. When the L&Y and LNW Railway amalgamated in 1922, he became Signal Engineer, Manchester. Bound would have been very happy to have Berry as his assistant, but being a chronic arthritic, he chose to retire, which he did on 31st October 1929. He was president of the IRSE in 1929 and died in France on 21st April 1931.*

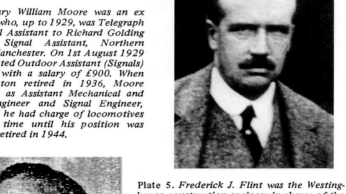

Plate 4. *Henry William Moore was an ex L&YR man, who, up to 1929, was Telegraph and Electrical Assistant to Richard Golding Berry, the Signal Assistant, Northern Division at Manchester. On 1st August 1929 he was appointed Outdoor Assistant (Signals) Derby (HQ) with a salary of £900. When A. S. Hampton retired in 1936, Moore replaced him as Assistant Mechanical and Electrical Engineer and Signal Engineer, Glasgow, and he had charge of locomotives for a short time until his position was clarified. He retired in 1944.*

Plate 5. *Frederick J. Flint was the Westinghouse construction engineer in charge of the power scheme. He was a native of Gosforth and came south to Watford and, on leaving school, joined the LNWR in the Signal Department. Following service in the Royal Horse Artillery, he returned to the LNWR before joining Westinghouse in 1926 at 1/8d per hour. After a few months he was made a leading wireman but his abilities soon got him promotion and in 1928 he was placed in charge of his first big contract – Manchester Victoria & Exchange. He was also involved with the LMS ARP signal boxes at Crewe North and South. He retired to Bude and in 1969 the author had the privilege of meeting him.*

WESTINGHOUSE

passed through Manchester Victoria and Exchange owing to the lack of platform accommodation' etc.

Plans were tabled which included:

1. A proposal to modify Oldham Road Goods station to deal with fish traffic which was dealt with on the site of the old station between Victoria and Exchange stations, thus freeing up the site to be used for 'improved platform and running facilities'.
2. A proposal to lengthen the platforms at Exchange and alter connections to assist the marshalling of trains and shunting movements.
3. A proposal to provide additional junctions 'to link up Salford on the former Lancashire and Yorkshire system and Ordsall Lane on the former London and North Western line with either Manchester Victoria or Exchange Stations'.
4. A proposal to make Victoria and Exchange Stations 'closed' as currently Exchange was an 'open' station.
5. A proposal 'that No. 11 platform at Victoria be extended to the west end of Exchange No. 3 platform, with an additional running road from which trains could be turned into either of three sections of the new platform, which arrangement would greatly assist in dealing with the heavy holiday traffic, as the passengers would be able to gain access to the platform either from the existing Victoria Station, Exchange Station or the suggested new entrance opposite the Hunt's bank Offices'.

The cost of the above work was estimated to be £177,243, the scheme being approved by the committee and referred to the General Purposes Committee.

There was no mention of colour light re-signalling in the above proposals, as such signalling was very much in its infancy at this time.

It should also be remembered that road competition was creeping in and economies had to be sought and pursued wherever possible; the elimination of signal boxes would result in staff and wage reductions. Several schemes came up for consideration, which, if mechanical signalling was retained, would require a number of new signal boxes to be built. The decision was therefore made to remove all the mechanical signalling and replace with a system of power operation.

Briefly, the work embraced the following, which satisfied the Traffic Minute 246 above:

1. The provision of additional up and down crossover double junctions at Deal Street for intercommunication between the North (late L&Y) and South (late LNWR) lines; also up and down crossover double junctions at Ordsall Lane between the slow and fast lines.
2. The remodelling of Victoria West Junction and alterations between that point and the east end of Exchange station, in order to provide a through

down line formed by linking No. 16 road Victoria (No. 11 platform) with No. 3 platform road Exchange station. (This platform became the longest in Europe, quoted in the *LMS Magazine* to be 2,238 feet long, and was officially opened on 16th April 1929 by Miss Edna Best the then current 'Railway Queen'. The *Railway Year Book* for 1958/9 states the platform is 2194 feet long?)

3. The remodelling of the connections of all lines at the west end of Exchange Station consequent upon the lengthening of No. 1, 2, 3 and 4 platforms in a westerly direction, and the provision of the new down through line referred to above.

4. To accomplish the foregoing, much civil work was involved, including widening the bridge over the River Irwell, other bridging work, as well as platform and roofing work.

When the above work was completed, it enabled trains to leave Victoria for destinations originally only served by the ex-LNWR (south) lines such as North Wales with trains able to leave Exchange for places in the north and west for which only Victoria was generally used. Such an improvement clearly saved many passengers having to transfer between stations.

The Manchester Victoria and Exchange scheme was the first extensive use of power signalling away from London, although we should not overlook some of the earlier schemes such as Newcastle-on-Tyne in 1904 when a compressed air system was installed which was electro pneumatic but still used mechanical type signals operated by air cylinders, and the 'Crewe' system of Webb and Thompson dating from 1898 when mechanical type signals were operated by electric solenoids.

THE CONTRACT

Four contractors were invited to tender for the re-signalling, with the Westinghouse Brake and Saxby Signal Co. Ltd. being awarded the contract in November 1927; their quotation was £64,892 which was reduced by £2,000 when the LMS decided to use its own staff as look-out men. The LMS were required to carry out work estimated at £24,011, making a total cost of £86,903. The LMS estimate was £85,230 that was very close. Westinghouse were also required to take out an insurance policy to cover any accidents that might occur as a result of their operations for up to £30,000 for any one accident. The work was completed in March 1929. Permanent way alterations were carried out by the LMS, who, using a local firm, built the signal boxes. The signal foundations were also prepared by the railway company, some using pre-cast bases. The signals were designed and manufactured by Westinghouse in their Chippenham works, the exception being the gantries, which were constructed externally to Westinghouse designs.

All signals were erected by Westinghouse as were the point machines, power frames, cables, relays, cabinets, rectifiers, etc. A. Reyrolle acted as sub-contractors in supplying the 400 volt switchgear for controlling the supply to the transformers and rectifiers.

Messrs. S. & J. Smethurst successfully tendered for the steelwork required for the three new signal boxes – Victoria East Junction, Deal Street and Irwell Bridge Sidings, the cost being £1,078 14s. 3d.

Works Committee Minute 1889 dated 22nd May 1929 reported the scheme was completed. The total cost of the signalling scheme was £88,647.

The Manchester scheme was 'all electric' and the work covered the line between Ordsall Lane No. 2 Signal Box/Oldfield Road No. 1 signal Box and Manchester Victoria East Junction Signal Box. Two new signal boxes were built together with one ground frame, totalling 188 levers, replacing 332 levers installed in six signal boxes and one ground frame. It should also be remembered that the 188 levers worked many additional connections that did not previously exist. The term 'all-electric' requires clarification in that the Westinghouse style 'K' power frames were mechanically interlocked.

There were many features of the Manchester Victoria and Exchange scheme which were very interesting at the time, when it is considered that no standard practice was laid down in connection with colour light schemes and the engineers had to face various problems for the first time. Perhaps the main feature was that it was one of the first systems of power-operated points and colour light signals combined with full track circuit control.

OTHER CONTRACTS

The contract for the roof over the new platforms and the widening of the Irwell bridge was awarded to Messrs. E. Taylor & Co, whose amount of £47,355.1.5d was way over the Chief Engineer's estimate of £31,067. Works Committee Minute 756 (29th July 1925) decided to proceed with the contract providing a satisfactory explanation was given for the difference in the estimates. The Widnes Foundry (1925) Ltd. tender of £994 9s.0d was accepted for the widening of the Irwell bridge.

Five tenders were invited to strengthen the River Irwell bridge with reinforced concrete but none was received. However, Messrs. Mouchell & Partners submitted a price of £12,000 in addition to which they required two further amounts of 350 guineas for the design and supervision respectively. The LMS Chief Engineer stated the work could be done

Plate 6. *A single slip point machine with lock and detector in the 4ft way. The point machine was the Westinghouse M2 type requiring 110 volts DC. When locks and detectors were required in the 4ft with slip points, etc, the Westinghouse Style 'C' point and lock detectors were used, as in this case. The average time required to operate a pair of points was 2½ seconds taking 3½ amps.*

Plate 7. *A standard Westinghouse three-compartment apparatus case, reference Ka. 102, 202, being externally 4ft 6½in high x 3ft 2¼in wide, the internal width being 1ft. The case contained four relays for track circuits with terminal blocks. The wooden troughing behind was preserved using creosote which attacked the cable insulation, requiring the cable to be replaced at roughly 5-year intervals.*

for £11,000 by his own staff and this was agreed in Works Committee Minute 914 dated 24th February 1926. The original idea was to rebuild the bridge at a cost estimated at £16,000.

The *LMS Magazine* stated that it had been necessary to reinforce the old bridge and move a steel parapet girder, 142ft long weighing 85 tons, a distance of 32ft and build a steel girder of 100 tons weight on site. The alterations required 2,320 cubic yards of concrete, and, in the platform roof and windscreen, 37,120 superficial feet of glass was required.

SIGNAL BOXES

Fig. 2 shows the new and retained signal boxes together with those abolished which can be summarized as follows: three new signal boxes – Deal Street, Victoria West Junction and Irwell Bridge Sidings replaced seven mechanical signal boxes as below as listed in the *LMS Magazine* for June 1929:

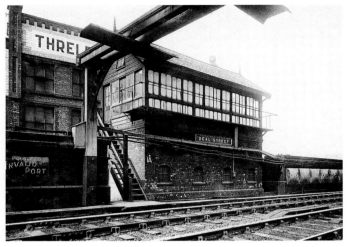

Plate 8. *Deal Street L&Y signal box containing 43 mechanical levers, which was replaced by the new Deal Street power box.*

Mechanical Levers		Power Levers	
Irwell Bridge	100	Victoria West Junction	85
Victoria West Junction	31		
Exchange No. 1	33		
Exchange No. 2	88	Deal Street	91
Deal Street	43		
Salford ex LNW	8		
Irwell Bridge Sidings	29	Irwell Bridge Sidings	12
Total Working Levers	**332**		**188**

Plate 9. *Salford LNW signal box containing eight mechanical levers, which was replaced by Deal Street power box.*

The Mechanical frames in the signal boxes adjoining the Manchester scheme were modified as follows:

Victoria East Junction – The number of mechanical levers was reduced to 81 working with 11 spare and 16 spaces; colour light signals and route indicators were provided in place of the incoming semaphore signals, the outgoing semaphores being retained.

Salford ex L&Y – the number of mechanical levers was reduced from 66 to 59 working levers with 9 spare and 24 spaces. The working levers were concentrated in the middle of the frame and track circuiting and colour light signals were installed on the fast and slow platform lines.

Ordsall Lane No. 2 – had its mechanical levers increased from 68 to 70 due to the laying of a new junction leading from the down slow to the down fast and also the working of the advanced starting signals from this box instead of Salford (LNW) as previously.

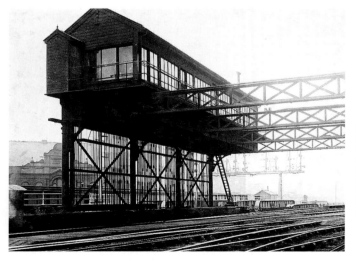

Plate 10. *Manchester Exchange No. 2 signal box is a fine example of an LNWR overhead signal box which contained 88 mechanical levers and was replaced by the new Deal Street power box.*

Plate 11. *Irwell Bridge L&Y overhead signal box containing 100 mechanical levers, which was replaced by Victoria West Junction power box.*

Plate 12. *The interior of Irwell Bridge L&Y overhead signal box containing 100 mechanical levers, which was replaced by Victoria West Junction power box.*

Fig. 2. *An outline diagram showing the work involved in the resignalling of Manchester Victoria & Exchange.*

1929 MANCHESTER VICTORIA & EXCHANGE RE-SIGNALLING.
DIAGRAM OF CONNECTIONS AND SIGNAL BOXES. NOT TO SCALE.

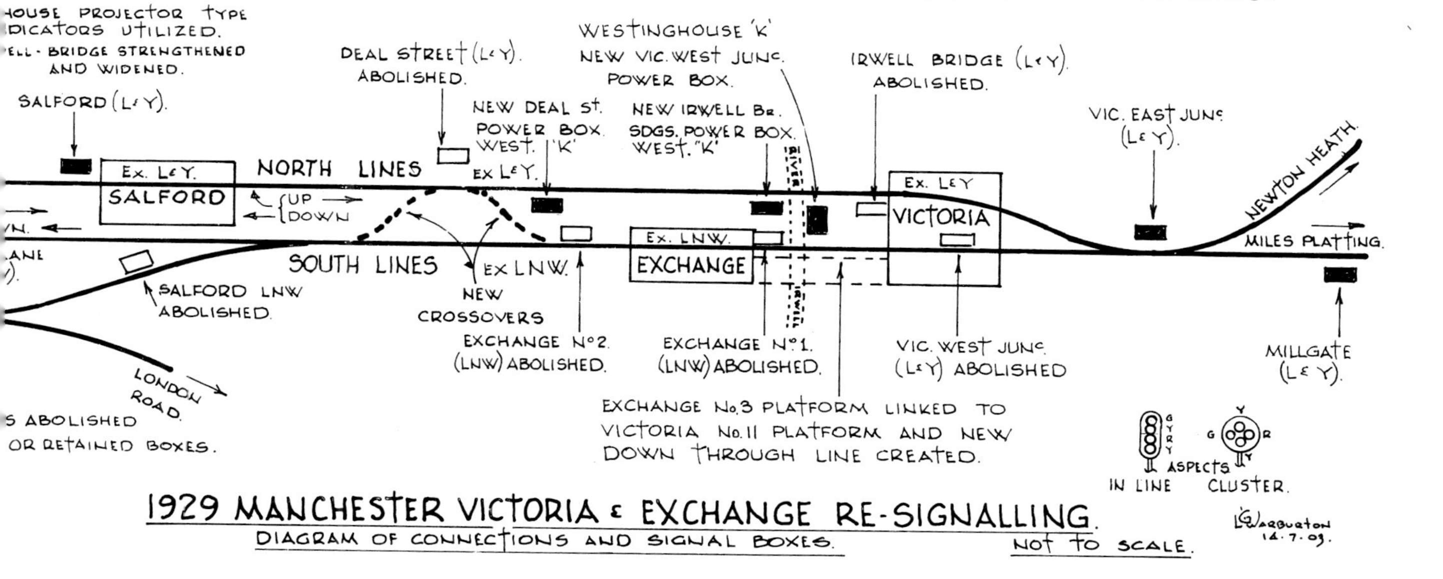

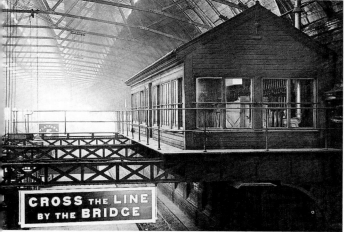

Plate 13. *Manchester Exchange No. 1 was an LNWR overhead box containing 33 mechanical levers, which was replaced by Victoria West Junction power box.*

Plate 14. *Victoria West Junction cabin containing 31 mechanical levers, replaced by Victoria West Junction power box.*

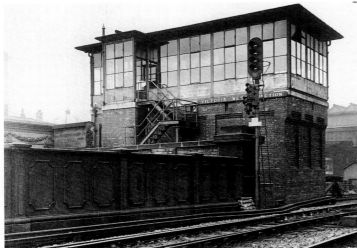

Plate 15. *The new Victoria West Junction signal box that replaced Irwell Bridge, Victoria West Junction and Exchange No. 1. The new box had 95 levers as follows: 50 signal levers, 31 point levers, 4 release levers and 10 spare. The signal was: V5 [ex 69] Victoria West Junction Down Main Intermediate Home; V6 [ex 70] ditto Calling-on; V7 [ex 71] ditto to Siding. Initially, signals were allocated a unique number from 1 to 215 and covered all the signal boxes involved, as shown on the drawing that accompanied the notice dated 22nd February 1929. Clearly the consecutive numbering of signals did not identify the controlling signal box and so all signals were renumbered to indicate the controlling signal box – e.g. D (Deal Street), S (Salford), etc. Both numbers are referred to on the photograph captions.*
WESTINGHOUSE

Plate 16. *Victoria West Junction Westinghouse style 'K' power frame (K33) with the block bells and block indicators below them, a green light indicating 'line clear' and a red light for 'train on line'; the 'line blocked' was signified by no light being lit. The electrical repeaters for the points and signals are seen above the levers. The points had a double indicator lettered 'N' (normal) and 'R' (reverse). Each signal had up to four indications, Red, Yellow, Yellow/Yellow and Green, dependent on the signal.*
WESTINGHOUSE

Plate 17. *Victoria West Junction Westinghouse style 'K' power frame with the block bells and block indicators below them, a green light indicating 'line clear' and a red light for 'train on line'; the 'line blocked' is signified by no light being lit. The electrical repeaters for the points and signals are seen above the levers. The points had a double indicator lettered 'N' (normal) and 'R' (reverse). Each signal had four indications 'R', 'Y', 'YY' and 'G'.*

Plate 18. *A Westinghouse wall-mounted bracket with 4-aspect colour light cluster signal, calling on signal and route indicator controlled by the new Victoria West Junction box. V28 [ex 188] Up Through Home with route indicator reading: To No. 3 Platform – indication '3'; To Down Through – indication 'T'; To No. 4 Platform – indication '4'. V29 [ex 189] Up Through Home 'Calling On'.*

THE POWER FRAMES

The Westinghouse Company had finalised the designs of their all-electric style 'L' frame that was first brought into use on the Southern Railway at North Kent East Junction (frame L37) on 1st December 1929. The Company tried hard to persuade the LMS to accept electric interlocks, but as their engineers consisted of a mechanical and an electrical engineer, there were two differing viewpoints (no doubt such differences were part of the reason leading to the formation of the consolidated Signal and Telegraph Department in 1929). This resulted in Manchester having some of the last Westinghouse style 'K' mechanically interlocked power frames to be installed in this country, all three of which were ordered in November 1927.

The last UK example went to Whitechapel (K36) with a further frame going to Brazil (K38) and two to the Bombay Baroda and Central India Railway (K62 & 64). The next large LMS power scheme at Glasgow St. Enoch had the third 'all-electric' Style 'L' frame (L45) to be made. The fundamental difference between the two types of power frame was that on the mechanically interlocked frame, all levers are free until the locking is put on, whilst on the electrically locked frame, all levers are locked until the releases are put on. We therefore have the lever interlocking on one side of the locks, and on the other the track locking and selection locking, thus proving the integrity of the whole system when a lever is free to be pulled. The later patterns of relay locking made this type of power frame obsolete.

Considerable economy in the number of working levers was made in all three boxes with the use of 'push and pull' arrangements and by selection. The use of 'push-pull' levers was in accordance with LMS Railway practice for shunt signals, the normal position of the 'push-pull' lever being in the centre of the quadrant with the two reverse positions being 'push' and 'pull'. Where power is employed for signal operation, there is no question of the length of stroke other than the amount required to break one contact and make another. The movement from the mid position to full reversed (pulled) or reversed to full normal (pushed) is sufficient, which was 60 degrees in the style 'K' frame.

Because of the 'push-pull' arrangement or by selection, only 53 levers were

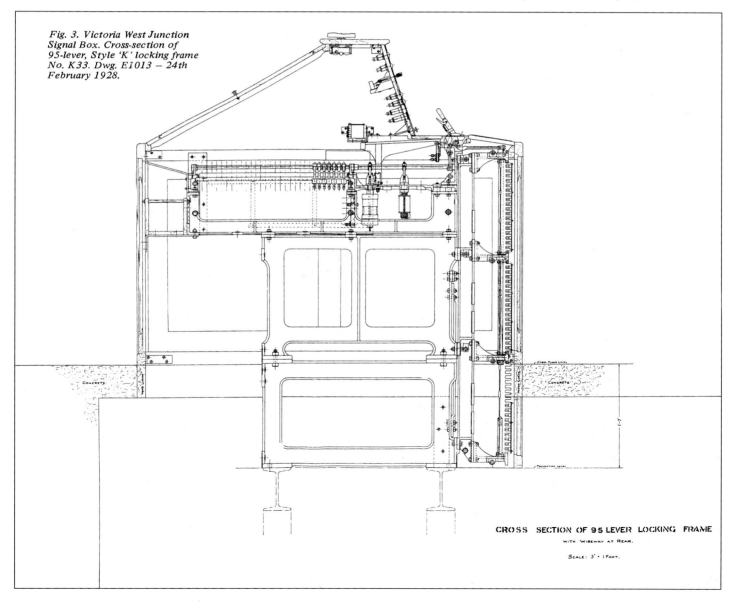

Fig. 3. Victoria West Junction Signal Box. Cross-section of 95-lever, Style 'K' locking frame No. K33. Dwg. E1013 – 24th February 1928.

Plate 19. *Looking west from platform 11 on Victoria station, the nearest signal on the platform was: 41 [ex 182] Victoria West Junction No. 16 Road Outer Home with route indicator reading To No. 16 Road – indication '16'; To Down Slow North – indication 'S'. 42 [ex 183] Victoria West Junction No. 16 Road 'Calling on'.*

Plate 20. *A four-aspect cluster signal together with a route indicator and 'Calling on' signal suspended from a gantry within Victoria ex-L&Y station. V30 [ex 180] Victoria West Junc. Up Main Intermediate Home; V31 [ex 181] Victoria West Junc. Up Main Intermediate Home – 'Calling on'. The route indicator read: To No. 16 Road – indication '16'; To Up Through – indication 'T'; To Up Main – indication 'M'.*

Plate 21. *Victoria West Junction signal box interior with a Westinghouse 'Style K' still in use 60 years after installation, on 19th July 1989. The signal box diagram had been updated with more white out-of-use levers in the frame and new lever plates provided.*

required for 77 signals at Deal Street, and at Victoria West Junction 50 levers were required for 80 signals, the ground frame requiring 4 levers for 12 signals; thus there were 107 levers for 169 signals. The use of 30 route indicators giving 80 indications in the two new boxes alone saved 50 more signals which would mostly have been of the four-aspect type. In total there were 192 signals (exclusive of distant signals) reading over 299 routes worked by 135 levers.

Behind the levers were the electrical repeaters for the points and signals. For points, a double indication was provided, N for normal and R for reversed. Every signal had an electrical repeater giving the four indications Yellow, Yellow/Yellow, Green and Red. A lever with a pull push movement, generally for a shunt or siding signal, had one red for the pull movement, one red for the push and one green for either signal being clear. Above the repeaters were the block instruments and behind the frame was the illuminated diagram. A feature of this was that when a train was ready to depart from any platform, the station staff pressed a switch on that platform which lit up the appropriate part of the diagram. A similar arrangement was made for vehicles left detached in the platform, by the inspector operating a switch, causing a lamp to be lit on the diagram in case a vehicle had failed to operate the track circuit. Where one box released the other, the signalman in one box pulled the appropriate lever, causing a white light to appear in the other box. When the other box accepted the release, the word 'free' was illuminated over the lever in the first box.

Victoria West Junction power frame (K33) comprised 41 full-stroke signal levers, 9 push/pull signal levers, 31 point levers, 4 release levers, 4 spare point levers, 6 spare signal levers, totalling 95 levers. A note on the Westinghouse drawing dated May 1932 indicates that 2 spare point levers (21 & 35) and 2 spare signal levers (20 & 34) were later brought into use.

Deal Street power frame (K34) comprised 48 full-stroke signal levers, 6 push/pull signal levers, 37 point levers, 1 switching out lever, 3 spare point levers, 4 spare signal levers, totalling 99 levers plus the spaces for eight more (four at each end). A note on the Westinghouse drawing, also dated May 1932, indicates that a spare signal push/pull lever No. 98 was

Plate 22. *The new Deal Street Signal Box equipped with 99 power levers that replaced Deal Street, Salford LNW and Exchange No. 2.* WESTINGHOUSE

Plate 23. *The interior of Deal Street Power Box showing the diagram and the 99-lever Westinghouse Style 'K' mechanically-locked power frame K34, consisting of 53 signal levers, 37 point levers, 1 switching-out lever, 8 spare levers and 8 spaces. Sometime later, levers were added to the left-hand A, B, C, D, spaces. The signal and point repeaters are seen immediately behind the levers and above them the repeaters for the route indicators. The block instruments are seen under the shelf on top of the locking frame.* WESTINGHOUSE

Plate 24. A new colour light signal gantry worked from Deal Street signal box looking towards Exchange Station with the new Deal Street signal box in the background. The designated south lines (ex LNW) are seen in the right of the picture and the north lines (ex L&Y) to the left. This picture was taken with the work still in progress as LMS flagmen can be seen on the right. The new cable trunking can be seen running down the centre of the picture, the point rodding to the right of which had yet to be removed. The turnout on the left gave access to the North down slow line from Irwell Bridge Sidings. The steelwork spanning the South lines was all that remained of Manchester Exchange No. 2 ex LNWR overhead signal box. Designation plates had still to be fitted to the two cluster signals on the top right-hand end of the gantry. Top left – D30 [ex 38] South line Up Slow Intermediate Home with R.I. reading: Up Slow [South] – indication 'S'; To No. 4 Platform – indication '4'; To Up Fast [South] – indication 'F'; D31 [ex 39] South line Up Slow Intermediate 'Calling on'. Top right – D41A [ex 60] South line Up Fast Intermediate Home; D41B [ex 61] South line Up Fast Intermediate Home to Down Fast South; D72 [ex 62] South line Up Fast Intermediate Home to Home 'Calling on'. Lower – 64C [ex 200] South line Down Inner Home to Slow North; 64B [ex 201] South line Down Inner Home to Fast South. The three-doll colour signal in the background was (from left to right): 24C [ex 164] North line Down Slow Home to Down Slow; 24A [ex 166] North line Down Slow Home to South line Down Slow.
WESTINGHOUSE

later brought into use, reducing the spare signal levers to three.

Irwell Bridge Sidings power frame (K35) comprised 4 signal levers, 8 point levers and 3 spare.

BLOCK WORKING

Block working was maintained throughout the whole area, but the Deal Street and Victoria West Junction instruments were let into the upper part of the front of the locking frame. The block signals were normally sent by a commutator, which moved from mid-position to the right to give 'line clear' and to the left to give 'train on line'. The block indications were given by a green light for 'line clear' and a red light for 'train on line'. 'Line blocked' was given by no light indication. Signals received were in the upper part and those sent in the lower. Not only was block working in force, but the instrument controlled the last stop signal of the signal box in the rear. A train on the last track circuit in advance de-energized a stick relay of the signal, and before the home relay controlling it could be energized, 'line clear' must have been given for the train. Should a lever be inadvertently pulled before 'line clear' was given, the relay would be energized. The designation of trains was given to Deal Street and Victoria West Junction by telephone.

Manchester was also unique in being the first place in the world to have luminous block instruments. With modern power signalling installations, the block telegraph is dispensed with although block bells are retained for emergencies.

ELECTRICITY SUPPLY

Manchester was the first place to have 3-phase AC supplies to the signal boxes. A substation was built at the west end of No. 1 platform of Exchange station, which took two 400 volt 50 cycle AC supplies from independent points of the Salford Corporation Electricity undertaking. In addition, a further supply was brought in as a standby from Manchester Corporation at 400 volts DC (it was not possible to obtain a third AC supply), which operated a 40 BHP motor-alternator set to give a 400 volt 3-phase 50 cycle supply in the event of the failure of the AC supplies. This arrangement was designed by The Harland Company Ltd. Under normal conditions, one AC supply fed the main busbars through oil circuit breakers and electrically-operated contactors. In the event of this

Plate 25. *A Westinghouse cantilever gantry signal adjacent to Deal Street signal box. 19C [ex 156] Deal Street North line Down Fast Home; 19B [ex 157] Deal Street North line Down Fast Home to Slow North; 19A [ex 158] Deal Street North line Down Fast Home to Slow South. D2 [ex 131] with route indicator reading: To Down Slow South – indication 'A'; To Down Slow North – indication 'S'; To Neck – indication 'N'; To Down Fast North – indication 'F'.*

Plate 26. *A Westinghouse bracket signal: D9 [ex 18] Deal Street north line up slow starter with route indicator reading: To No. 21 Road – indication '21'; To Down Main – indication 'T'.*

Plate 27. *A Westinghouse 4-aspect vertical type colour light signal on a single post with a 'calling on' signal and route indicator: D32 [ex 40] Deal Street South line Up Slow Inner Home with route indicator reading To Up Passenger Loop – indication 'L'; To No. 5 platform – indication '5'. D33 [ex 41] Deal Street South line Inner Home 'Calling on'. The signal in the background was D9 [ex 18] Deal Street North line Up Slow Starter with route indicator reading: To No. 21 Road – indication '21'; To Down Main – indication 'T'.*

Plate 28. *The new Irwell Bridge Sidings Power Box which replaced the old Irwell Bridge Sidings Signal Box which contained 29 mechanical levers.*
WESTINGHOUSE

Plate 29. *The interior of Irwell Bridge Power Box complete with Westinghouse Style 'K' 15-lever mechanically-locked power frame K35 of which three were spare with the diagram above.*
WESTINGHOUSE

failing, the second AC supply is switched in automatically, whilst should this also fail, the motor-alternator comes into action automatically through contact relays. From the substation, duplicate cables were run to the two main signal boxes at Deal Street and Victoria West Junction where switchgear cubicles were installed with appropriate transformer and rectifier sets. Westinghouse metal rectifiers of the copper oxide type supplied the direct current at 110 volts for point operation by Westinghouse machines.

The rectifiers were developed by Westinghouse from the original de Forest patents, and Manchester was the first installation of note to use this means of obtaining DC supplies from AC mains. There were duplicate sets of rectifiers in each of the main signal boxes, each of 3kw output, which were bridge connected from the 3-phase supply giving full wave rectification at a steady 110 volts DC of excellent regulation. What is interesting is that because so little was known about metal rectifiers in those days, they were given a six-monthly inspection, with some being sent to the laboratory for examination, but they were always found to be satisfactory.

The substation and its equipment were supplied by the LMS, with the signal box switchboards, transformers and rectifiers supplied and installed by Westinghouse.

CABLES AND TRUNKING

In total it was calculated that the equivalent of 33¼ miles of 'Maconite' 660 volt insulated conductor was used on the contract, with all the cable running round the interlocking carried in creosoted wooden trunking and troughing in accordance with the LMS specification. An estimated 10 miles of such trunking was laid. Experience later gained showed that the cable insulation was affected by the creosote, requiring the cables to be replaced approximately every seven years.

TRACK CIRCUITS

Track circuiting extended from Ordsall Lane and Salford to Victoria East, requiring 175 circuits ranging in length from 45 to 1,260 feet, totalling 11¾ track miles. They were of the AC condenser-fed type, a condenser being connected direct in one leg of the feed circuits, the relays being of

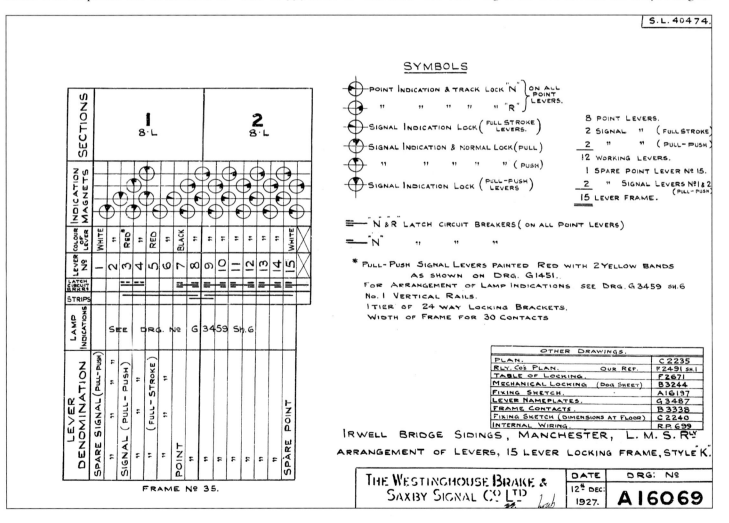

the double element vane type. For points they provided sectional release, approach locking, back locking and route locking. The 3-phase supply came in at 400 volts and was transformed down to 120 volts 3-phase. The 120 volt ring main on 3 phases was a great help in getting phase displacement on certain circuits where one phase could be used for the local and one phase for the track circuit itself. It was, however, discovered, when the system was brought into use, there were certain dangers only appertaining to three-position indicating relays where there was point detection of normal and reverse. This was the case in which phase displacement again occurred in the event of the white phase fuse blowing, when the red and blue phases reversed, throwing all the relays to their opposite function. Thereafter it was important to keep the detection circuits on the same phase.

Signal engineers in those days always had a fear of wrong side failures (and indeed they still do) in track circuits, several of which occurred at Manchester, which were traced to filling locomotive sand boxes with Blackpool sand which included a multiplicity of minute shells, occasionally forming a perfect insulator between wheels and rails, especially with lightweight vehicles.

A further innovation of this scheme, which had not been used hitherto on systems of 'lock and block', was a feature developed by Westinghouse known as 'sectional release route locking', which meant that if a route was set up across a whole sequence of points which fouled other routes, as the train cleared the clearing points, a release was obtained to replace the signals and points which could be re-pulled, enabling other safe moves to be made. The old system used either treadles or electric depression bars, and once a train had passed a signal, the lever could not be replaced until the last vehicle was clear of the route set up, which in some cases was over many sets of points, thus holding up other traffic, especially when this system operated at very busy interlocked areas.

RUNNING LINE SIGNALS

The colour light signals were mainly of the 4-aspect type arranged vertically or as a cluster. In certain positions, such as entering platform roads, a 3-aspect vertical or cluster signal was provided, which, due to low speeds, gave no clear (green) indication. There were also 2-aspect vertical type signals fixed at the entrance to a station platform giving stop (red) or caution (yellow) only. There were 88 four-aspect, 3 three-aspect and 3 two-aspect running signals, 36 route indicating signals, 27 calling-on signals, 66 two-aspect and 2 two-aspect ground signals. See *Fig. 5* for details of all the various signal aspects on this scheme. Four- and three-aspect cluster signals were provided when they acted as splitting signals at a junction and also to get

Plate 30. *Manchester Victoria and Exchange electricity substation situated at the west end of No. 1 platform. Two 400 volt AC supplies came from Salford Corporation and one 400 volt DC supply came from Manchester Corporation. The signal was D89 [ex 210] No. 1 Road Inner Home with route indicator reading: To Down Fast (South) – indication 'F'; To Down Fast (South) via Up Fast (South) – indication 'F'; To Down Slow (South) – indication 'S'.*
ROY ANDERSON

them as low as possible when on a bracket or bridge.

The illumination of each aspect of the running signal was by double filament lamps of 6 volt and 12 watts per filament, the inner lenses being of the 8in diameter Fresnal type. To enable drivers to satisfactorily observe the signal when stopped close to it, there was a device called an auxiliary light deflecting unit consisting of a small lens placed between the Fresnal lens and the outer plain lens to give a bright indication on the side of the signal head approximately 2¼in diameter. The range under normal conditions of sunlight for a running signal was from 2500 feet to 5000 feet, the light spread being approximately 5 degrees.

Of further interest was the introduction of a system of light signalling into an area controlled by mechanical signals at either end. At the entering end of the light signal area, a colour light distant signal was installed below the semaphore stop arm, the indication being no light when the arm is at danger. When the mechanical arm is pulled 'off', the electrically-lit signal lamp is switched out, switching on the colour light signal that will display yellow, double yellow or green, dependent on the conditions ahead.

The lines to Manchester are designated Up, with those from Manchester designated Down, the dividing line being across the station, just east of Irwell Bridge Siding Signal Box between the two stations. This means that a train arriving from the Salford or Ordsall Lane side, arrives on a designated Up line and departs on to Newton Heath or Miles Platting on a designated Down line.

Initially signals were allocated a unique number from 1 to 215 and covered all the signal boxes involved, as shown on the drawing that accompanied the notice dated 22nd February 1929. Clearly the consecutive numbering of signals did not identify the controlling signal box and so all signals were re-numbered to indicate the controlling signal box – e.g. D (Deal Street); S (Salford), etc. Both numbers are referred to on the photograph captions.

SEMI-AUTOMATIC RUNNING LINE SIGNALS

Semi-Automatic Advanced Starting signals were provided on the up and down fast and slow lines between Ordsall Lane and Deal Street signal boxes with telephones. If a driver was brought to a stand at any of these signals, he telephoned the signalman, advising him of his waiting train. If the signal was working correctly, the signalman advised the driver to await the 'proceed' aspect, but if the apparatus had failed, the driver was instructed to pass the signal at danger, proceeding slowly, and be prepared to stop short of any obstruction. If the telephone was out of order, the driver was to remain at the signal for three minutes before proceeding as above; he was also to stop at the next signal box in advance, advising the signalman of the telephone breakdown.

Salford Station box could be switched out, the signals working automatically, and, in the event of failure, the three-minute rule applied, the driver notifying Deal Street box of the circumstances. The signals were replaced to danger after the engine had passed a distance varying from 25 to 100 feet beyond the signal. This was later revised, as at Glasgow St. Enoch, to 'last wheel replacement', sometimes known as the 'last wheel feature'. This meant that the signal reverted to red by forward track circuit occupied and rear track circuit cleared, the reason being to prevent signals going to red until passed by the banking or propelling engine, a feature also used at Liverpool Lime Street and halfway up the Lickey incline. The signals on the photographs which accompany this article carry identification plates referencing them to the controlling signal box. The LMS special notice dated 22nd February 1929, which brought the scheme into use, showed each signal having a unique number; both have been given on the relevant captions.

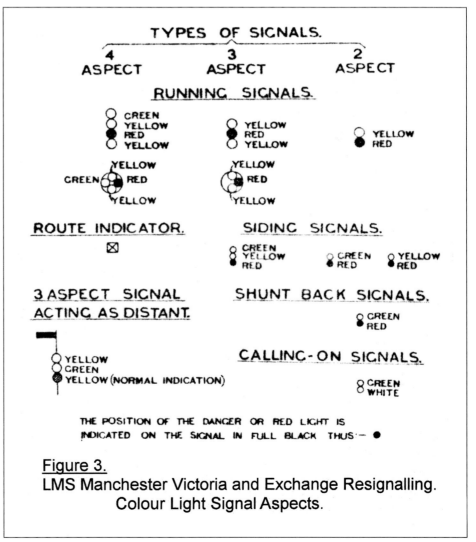

Figure 3.
LMS Manchester Victoria and Exchange Resignalling. Colour Light Signal Aspects.

Fig. 5. Colour light signal aspects.

Plate 31. *A fine example of a Westinghouse cantilever bracket signal supporting 2 & 4-aspect vertical colour light signals, 'calling on' signals and a route indicator. The right-hand signals were: V75 [ex 10] Victoria West Junction north line up fast home with route indicator reading: To No. 24 Road – indication '24'; To No. 23 Road – indication '23'; To No. 21 Road – indication '21'; V77 [ex 11] Victoria West Junction north line up fast home – 'Calling on'. The left-hand signals were: 89 [ex 153] Victoria West Junction north line down fast inner home; 78 [ex 154] Victoria West Junction north line down fast inner home to sidings – controlled from Irwell Bridge Sidings. See Fig. 6 below for a drawing of this signal. The ground mounted shunt back signals were: Front – V80B [ex 93] Victoria West Junction – along down fast north; Rear – V80A [ex 92] Victoria West Junction – down fast north to up fast.*
WESTINGHOUSE

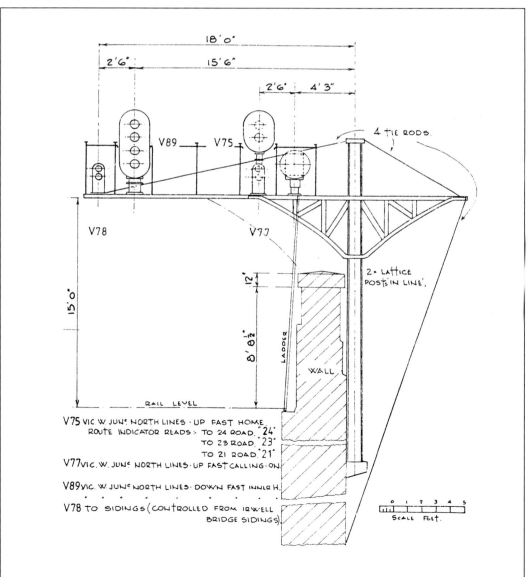

Fig. 6. Victoria West signals V75, V78, V79 and V89 (see Plate 31 above), from LMS Dwg. 1733 – 6th August 1928.

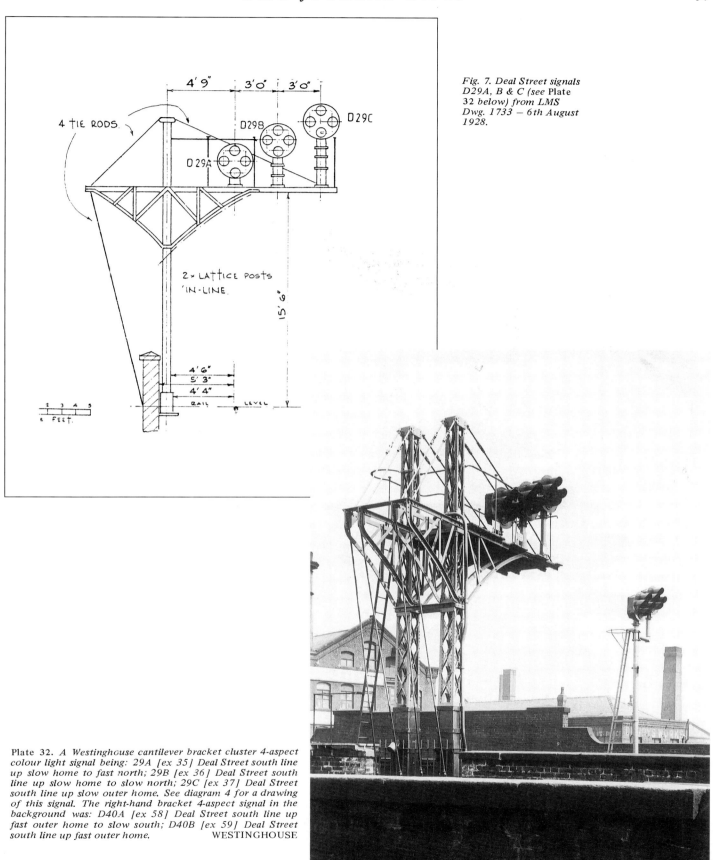

Fig. 7. Deal Street signals D29A, B & C (see Plate 32 below) from LMS Dwg. 1733 – 6th August 1928.

Plate 32. *A Westinghouse cantilever bracket cluster 4-aspect colour light signal being: 29A [ex 35] Deal Street south line up slow home to fast north; 29B [ex 36] Deal Street south line up slow home to slow north; 29C [ex 37] Deal Street south line up slow outer home. See diagram 4 for a drawing of this signal. The right-hand bracket 4-aspect signal in the background was: D40A [ex 58] Deal Street south line up fast outer home to slow south; D40B [ex 59] Deal Street south line up fast outer home.* WESTINGHOUSE

Plate 33. *The Victoria East Junction semaphore gantry of L&Y starting signals and the single-post signal to the right were retained under the resignalling scheme, as was the five-arm L&Y tall siding signal in the background, together with the signal box. The box can just be seen in the background to the left of signal VE13/14. The colour 4-aspect colour light signals were: VE13 [ex 176] Up South Home with Route Indicator reading: No. 16 road – indication '16', To Through – indication 'T', Up Main – indication 'S', No. 20 road – indication '20', No. 21 road – indication '21'; VE14 [ex 177] Up South Home 'Calling on'; (Note the 'D' sign attached to the signal post with its attendant L&Y type of Fireman's Call Box in the foreground centre of the picture); VE66 [ex 140] Up North Home with route indicator reading: No. 20 road – indication '20', No. 22 road – indication '22'; VE67 [ex 141] Up North Home 'Calling on'. There was also a 'D' sign on the post.* WESTINGHOUSE

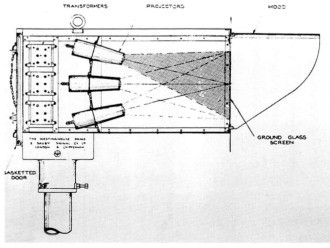

Plate 34. *Drawing showing a section through the Westinghouse Optical Route Indicator that had no moving parts, the image being projected onto a ground glass screen.* WESTINGHOUSE

Plate 35. *The Westinghouse 12in Optical Route Indicator.* WESTINGHOUSE

ROUTE INDICATORS

As stated, there were 36 route indicating signals of the Westinghouse optical projector type *(Plates 34 & 35)*, each of which was capable of giving 13 indications, although the maximum given at Manchester was 5, with the majority having 3 or 4. When a signal was changed from the 'stop' position, the lamp for the indicator was switched on and the appropriate letters or numerals were reflected through the stencil onto a screen by 12 volt 48 watt lamps, there being no moving parts.

The whole scheme lay roughly east to west, which, due to low sun in the morning and evening, made things a little awkward in the early days of colour light signalling, especially as the route indicators were of the optical type, which, being a type of bioscope, projected a number or letter on to a ground glass screen. The optical type was not used after this, the theatre type being preferred.

CALLING-ON SIGNALS

Calling-on signals were two-aspect signals of reduced size, exhibiting either a white or green light that were fixed under or near the main signal. White was the location light and green indicated 'proceed cautiously as far as the line is clear, or to the next signal only'. One peculiar incident which happened many times, and which could have brought colour light signalling into contempt by drivers, was the question of the calling-on indications on the long platform linking Victoria with Exchange. These were signals controlled from two signal boxes, resulting in Victoria West Junction clearing a call-on signal, and Deal Street, which, having had a train accepted by Ordsall Lane, pulled 'off' the first signal in his section, which could be considered to be his home signal, resulting in the call-on leading up to a green light.

This prompted signal engineers to query as to exactly what is a call-on signal? This was eventually defined by A.F. Bound, the LMS Signal and Telegraph Engineer, 'as being a signal that could only be used by a train having approached it, going into an occupied section ahead and it must always be controlled by those features that it should never be possible to give a call-on leading up to a clear section'. Drivers also frequently mistook the yellow lights for calling-on indications and

Plate 36. S65 *[ex 3]* Salford North Line Up Fast Home signal was a Westinghouse 4-aspect vertical colour light repeated at low level for sighting purposes. The picture was taken looking towards Manchester Victoria on the ex L&Y lines designated north lines under the resignalling scheme. Salford station is seen in the background together with the ex L&Y signal box that was retained as well as all the semaphore signals in the picture. Salford LNWR box was replaced by the new Deal Street box. The colour light gantry on the extreme right spanned the south, ex LNW lines.
WESTINGHOUSE

passed signals at danger, this being due to their inexperience with colour light signalling.

The two aspects of the calling-on signals and of the 2- and 3-aspect shunt or siding signals had an outer lens and also four smaller inner lenses in one frame. The former was frosted on the internal surface and behind each of the small lenses was a 12/14 volt 9 watt lamp, that is four lamps in each aspect.

SHUNT BACK SIGNALS
These were two-aspect signals exhibiting either a red or green indication, red being stop and the green 'proceed as far as the line is clear, or to the next signal only'.

SIDING SIGNALS
These were also two-aspect signals exhibiting either a red or green (except for one signal at Irwell Bridge Sidings which had a red and yellow light) or three-aspect signals exhibiting a red, yellow or green. The meaning of the aspects was the same as the shunt back signal, the yellow indicating the signal 'may be passed when performing shunting duties in sidings'.

POINT MACHINES
Westinghouse style 'M2' 110 volt DC machines taking 3.5 amps were utilised, combining lock and detection in one unit. Each switch of the points is electrically detected and, should a facing point lock be provided, it is detected independently. In all there were 130 point layouts, controlled by 128 point machines. Westinghouse style 'C' point and lock detectors were used in a number of cases such as double slips, etc, when it was required to fit locks and detectors in the 4-foot way. The average time for the operation of a pair of points was 2½ seconds, but the machine could also be hand operated via a crank handle in cases of emergency.

RULE 55
Apart from sounding the whistle, rule 55 was not applicable to colour light signals on this scheme except Victoria East Junction Home signals, Ordsall Lane No. 2 Up fast and Slow Outer Homes.

THE MINISTRY OF TRANSPORT INSPECTION
The MOT inspections were carried out on behalf of the Ministry of Transport by Lt. Col. A. H. L. Mount, affectionately referred to as 'Granny Mount' by A. F. Bound, presumably on account of him being a bit of an 'old woman' at times. In retrospect it must have been difficult for

Plate 37. *A Westinghouse M2 110 volt point machine working a British Standard point with 95lb rail and undercut switch. The track circuit plate reads Manchester No. 1927. In all, there were 130 point layouts controlled by 128 point machines. The gantry is seen at* Plate 16 *and the signal box in the background was Deal Street (*Plate 6*).*

WESTINGHOUSE

inspectors, generally having an army background and used to regulations and abiding by 'the book', to be constantly confronted by innovations introduced at this time by signal engineers endeavouring to take the science of railway signalling forward, particularly in respect of colour light and power signalling.

The Manchester scheme was inspected on 27th/28th February, 7th/8th March and 26th May 1929. Apart from certain reservations which necessitated the re-arrangement of the warning and calling-on arms in the colour light area, the Colonel was impressed, stating 'such an extensive installation reflected much credit on all concerned'. He remarked that one minute had been gained for the movement of traffic between Ordsall Lane and Exchange and between Salford and Victoria. The modifications requested were carried out by Westinghouse for £2,062.

FINALLY

The whole scheme was brought into use in three stages detailed in the LMS Special Notice dated 22nd February 1929 as follows:

On Sunday, 10th March 1929, commencing at 12.1am, the semaphore signals for the up and down fast and slow lines between Salford and Victoria Station (L&Y) side were dispensed with, along with the existing Victoria Deal Street and Irwell Bridge Signal Boxes, with colour light signalling introduced. The new Deal Street and the new Victoria West Junction boxes were brought into use so far as that section of line was concerned. All points worked from the existing boxes were then worked from the new boxes. The old Irwell Bridge Sidings Box was replaced by the new box of the same name.

The old L&Y West Junction Signal Box was temporarily renamed Victoria Station.

On Sunday, 17th March 1929, commencing at 12-1am, the semaphore signals for the up and down fast and slow lines between Ordsall Lane and the east end of Manchester (Exchange) were dispensed with, together with the existing Salford (LNW) and Manchester (Exchange) Nos. 2 & 1 Signal Boxes, with new colour light signalling introduced, worked from the existing Ordsall Lane No. 2, and the new Victoria Deal Street, and West Junction Signal Boxes. All the points worked from Exchange No. 2 Signal Box, together with

Plate 38. *A double slip power-worked point with the old mechanical signal box in the background.*

the new junctions between the north and south up and down slow lines and the new facing connection leading from the up fast to Nos. 1 and 2 platforms at Exchange station, being worked from the new Victoria Deal Street Signal Box. The points at the east end of Manchester (Exchange) were worked from the new Victoria West Junction Signal Box.

On Sunday, 24th March 1929, commencing at 12-1am, the semaphore signals worked by the Victoria Station Signal Box, together with the up fast and slow line semaphore signals from Footbridge direction, and up north and up south semaphore signals from the direction of Millgate, worked by Victoria East Junction Signal Box, were dispensed with and colour light signalling introduced. Victoria Station Signal Box was dispensed with. The junction at that place was re-arranged and worked from the new Victoria West Junction Box.

In order to do this, all drivers and guards who had signed for routes into Manchester Victoria and Exchange were conducted around the site before the new signals were brought into use. The scheme, when implemented required eleven less signalmen.

In 1944, the LMS S&T Department prepared a report entitled 'Colour Light Principles and Practice as applied by the London Midland and Scottish Railway 1929 to 1944'. The report considered what the company had achieved in that field and reviewed all the previously installed colour light schemes, making recommendations to bring these into line with standard practice gained by experience, and doubtless noting schemes that the SR and LNER had carried out over the previous ten years or so.

As far as Manchester Victoria and Exchange was concerned, the following was suggested:

1. There was one situation where it was considered there was insufficient stopping distance for express trains, and accordingly a third cautionary aspect of yellow over green be provided, meaning 'Attention pass second signal at restricted speed'. Such signals were in use at Mirfield, a scheme that will be described in a future issue of *LMS Journal*.
2. The two-aspect subsidiary units be replaced by the LMS standard position light signal.

Interestingly, although the ground shunting signals were non-standard, they were to be retained as the colours red, yellow and green were correctly displayed. I cannot state whether these recommendations were ever carried out.

As with all signalling, modifications were made over the years, such as the replacement of the cluster light signal heads with standard four-aspect in-line heads in the 1980s. Victoria West Junction closed on 8th August 1993, coming under the extended area of Victoria East Power Signal Box that was brought into use on 2nd April 1962. Deal Street closed on 31st July 1998 when replaced by the Manchester North Signalling Centre, with Irwell Bridge Sidings taken out of use earlier on 13th March 1988.

Acknowledgements

Railway Gazette.
The LMS Magazine.
Westinghouse Brake & Signal Company, Kevin Williams, Jill Darby and John Francis.
F. Flint – Westinghouse Signal Engineer.
W. J. Sadler, LMS Signal Engineer.
Ministry of Transport Report.

```
                L.M.S. HOTEL SERVICES,              TELEPHONE:
                                                    NORTH 4600.
                                                    TELEGRAMS:
                OFFICE OF THE CONTROLLER,           "TOWLAMID," LONDON.

  ARTHUR TOWLE,          FHA/MS.      ST. PANCRAS, LONDON, N.W. 1.
  CONTROLLER L.M.S.   My Ref. 21/H/306/S.
  HOTEL SERVICES
ST. PANCRAS, LONDON, N.W. 1.  Your Ref..............     21st. May, 1925.

  Miss G. Mann,
  28, Hartington Terrace,
  Lidget Green,
  BRADFORD.

  Madam,
          Further to my letter of the 17th. ulto., I can
  offer you a temporary position as Junior Housekeeper at the
  Midland Grand Hotel, St.Pancras, at a commencing salary of
  £65. per annum.
          As it is necessary that this appointment should
  be made at an early date, I shall be glad to hear from you by
  return.
                              Yours truly,
                              FOR ARTHUR TOWLE.

N.B.—Please address letters "Arthur Towle" and quote reference.
```

LMS HOTEL SERVICES

by BOB ESSERY

LMS Journal contributor Derek Ashworth sent this letter to me, suggesting that I might find a use for it. Arthur Towle was the Controller of LMS Hotel Services and an ex-Midland Railway employee but it is not possible to make out the signature of the person who signed the letter. Miss Mann, who lived in Bradford, was being offered a temporary position as a Junior Housekeeper at the Midland Grand Hotel, St. Pancras, but apart from her salary of £65 per annum, no other details were given. The questions that spring to mind are: was it a live-in post or did she have to find lodgings? What were her hours of work, did she get any particular day off, did the railway company send her a free pass to enable her to travel to London, or was this her responsibility?

This letter prompts the thought that we have never investigated the rates of pay for the lower grades of staff employed by the railway companies or their conditions of employment. Whilst I can clearly recall the rates paid to cleaners, firemen and drivers c.1948, any comparisons of pay rates have to be set against those that were applicable elsewhere at a given time.

Our accompanying picture of St. Pancras station and the Midland Grand Hotel was taken a little before Miss Mann moved from Bradford to London.

OF ENGINES AND ENGINEMEN
by KEITH MILES

Nothing more depressing for a Running Foreman coming on duty than to find the shed all but empty and the ashpit lined with dead or dying engines awaiting disposal. However, 'A Motive Power Depot must obtain agreement of the Control Room before ordering special enginemen for disposal of engines or other Motive Power duties' ERO 52457.   F. MORTON/ROWSLEY ASSOCIATION

VETERAN driver 'Kye' Gilbert, musing over a cup of tea in his retirement, opined, "It were a marvellous shed, were Rowsley. There wasn't a shed on t'system as worked as well, neither for th'engines nor men. Any engine was scheduled to do two days work in one; marvellous, I tell thee." Much as I applaud his partisan comment, it should be said that the diagrams, the common title for Engine & Enginemen's Workings, strived to achieve this throughout "t'system". These were compiled in the Divisional Trains Offices in association with each issue of the Working Timetables. I much regret that, while I worked alongside Cyril Cant, Roster Clerk, and Charlie Hartwell, Running Foreman, at Willesden in 1949 and was, myself, Running Foreman at Rowsley from the end of 1950 to 1955, I failed to keep any contemporary copies of these precious documents that had passed before me on a daily basis. I've since acquired odd examples from various places, but I'm pleased to say that a complete Rowsley set for the period commencing 12th September 1960 has been made available courtesy of Laurence Knighton of the Rowsley Association.

However, 'to begin at the very beginning', as somebody once said, and referring to Harold Rudgard's *Motive Power Organization and Practice*, ERO 53984; 'The Chief Operating Manager is the officer responsible for the whole of the Operating Department. The Superintendent of Motive Power is responsible to the Chief Operating Manager and Chief Mechanical Engineer for the Motive Power Section, his responsibilities being to provide the necessary Motive Power of suitable types and in good condition to work the requirements of the Traffic Section.' These responsibilities devolved upon the four Divisional Motive Power Superintendents at Derby (Midland), Crewe (Western), Manchester; (Central), and Glasgow (Northern), each of whom had three Assistants, General, Maintenance and Utilization. The latter's duties included 'engine supply and allocation with proper utilization' and 'economic utilization of enginemen and efficiency in link rostering.' My bosses at the Crewe Divisional Office in 1950 were C. R. Campbell, irreverently dubbed 'Ross Pop', with his Assistants, N. R. Peach (General), H. E. Fairhead (Maintenance) and W. J. Legg (Utilization) who I was later to come across again as the Depot Accommodation & Equipment Assistant at the Regional Motive Power Superintendent's Office, Euston, in 1955.

The provision of engine power was further devolved upon the District Motive Power Superintendents, of whom mine had been C. R. L. Rice at Willesden and W. (Bill) Bramley at Derby for Rowsley. Their duty was

> 'to see that locomotive power of the right classification and in good mechanical condition is supplied from each of the Sheds in his Area to meet the laid down demands necessary for traffic purposes, and to provide a measure of reserve power to meet the demands of Specials, and, in addition, to provide the necessary Enginemen with a knowledge of the road to operate the services. An allocation of power is made from the Divisional Motive Power Headquarters to the Area, the principle being that the Garage Depots normally will have sufficient engines to meet their diagrammed requirements, with a reasonable measure to cover Specials. The main reserve of engine

power should be at the Concentration Depot, and engines requiring heavy examinations or repairs which it is anticipated would necessitate their being out of service for periods exceeding twenty-four hours should be brought to the Concentration Depot for attention, a suitable engine being loaned to the Garage Shed where necessary to take its place.'

At the bottom of the pile but, nevertheless, at the sharp end, were the Running Foremen. Saving my blushes, I turn to Harry Webster and his *Locomotive Running Shed Practice*, Oxford University Press, 1947:

'The work of this grade is of the utmost importance to the efficient working of the depot and more dependence is probably placed upon the Running Foremen for that end than upon any other of the entire depot staff. Between them the three cover the 24 hours, working eight-hour shifts, so that no depot of any size is ever without a Running Foreman on duty. Running Foremen are responsible for the whole of the work performed by the shed grades from the time that an engine enters the loco yard until it leaves again ready for further service. These many duties, however, though extensive and important, are all secondary to his chief occupation which is to provide, from the engine stock available, the power required by the Operating Department for working trains.'

Put more prosaically in ERO 53984: 'The purpose of a Running Shed and its staff, from the District Locomotive Superintendent downwards, is to provide engines of the correct class, at the booked times, in the best possible mechanical condition, and manned by suitable engine crews, to work trains which they are booked to work without difficulty or delay on the road.'

The crucial part of Webster's commentary is 'from the engine stock available'. Timekeeping of freight trains in the 1950s was not at its best and engines and crews were very often late in getting back to the shed. Nothing was more depressing for a Running Foreman coming on duty, especially for a night shift, than to find the shed all but empty and the ashpit lined with dead or dying engines awaiting disposal. It was then a case of all hands to the pump, purloining men from wherever they could be found, even unoccupied Control Relief sets, to clear up the mess.

Anyway, back to diagrams: Rudgard's thoughts on the matter are as shown in the accompanying panel. In passing, elsewhere in his book he noted that 'Foremen appointed in a Motive Power Depot have been referred to as W. E. (Working Engines) Foremen and R. E. (Repairing Engines), Foremen, and it should be explained that these are terms which have been used for these grades over a long number of years although the correct staff list grade is Running Foreman or Running Shift Foreman and Foreman Fitter'. But to continue, Engine & Enginemen's Workings basically took three forms:

1. Engine Workings Only that covered locomotives manned sequentially by different sets of men, including 'foreigners' (i.e. from other depots) and also those moving outside the immediate area. Some extended to several days work with the appropriate number of engines; these were known as cyclical diagrams.
2. Engine & Men's Workings that, by and large, embraced one engine and one set of men for a day's work. It is the case, however, that some turns were linked, as with, for example, shunting engines.
3. Enginemen's Workings Only allowed for more than one engine-only working to be involved, again including 'foreigners', but also encompassing sets confined to the shed (preparing, disposing, etc.) and those for Control Relief.

A typical example of a cyclical diagram involving three 4F 0–6–0s, is that shown in the accompanying tabulated Rowsley turn 32. Briefly, on day one, Mondays excepted, the first engine banks the 4.51 Mineral to Buxton then returns light engine coupled. It later emerges from the shed to work the 12/2 Through Freight to Walton. On day two it works Walton's Target 120 for most of the day before returning to Rowsley on the 8/0 Express Freight from Huskisson. Meantime a second engine works the day one programme. On day three, the third engine enters the fray while the second engine advances to day two and the first engine works the 6.50 Through Freight to Chaddesden, returns to Rowsley on the 12/12 Mineral from Derby St. Mary's and finishes the day banking the 1/25 St.

(f) Engine Diagrams

Engine diagrams are prepared, in agreement with the Divisional Motive Power Assistant, at the Divisional Headquarters in the Trains Office, showing the detailed workings for each Shed and the class of engine which is booked to work the various trains.

The District Locomotive Superintendent must have a thorough knowledge of the diagrams in operation throughout his Area.

On receipt of new diagrams they should be closely scrutinized to ensure that they are correct from a practical working point of view, although they have previously been scrutinized by the Divisional Motive Power Assistant. Such points as short margins should be carefully watched, and if it is found in practice that any variation is considered desirable the matter should be taken up with the Divisional Office for an alteration to be effected.

Diagrams which break down, perhaps due to traffic requirements such as the detention of the engine in traffic from a previous portion of the working, should be taken up with Divisional Headquarters with a view to an alteration being made if nothing can be done locally with the District Operating Manager or Controller; the latter is responsible for all traffic operations within the agreed Area, and also for a considerable Traffic Staff within the Area, much in the same way as the District Locomotive Superintendent is on the mechanical side.

Both the District Locomotive Superintendent and the District Operating Manager or Controller come under the jurisdiction of the Divisional Operating Manager and very close contact should exist between the District Operating Manager or Controller and the District Locomotive Superintendents, and, of course, their Assistants.

The detailed duties of the R.E. and W.E. Foremen will be a later subject, but it is the responsibility of the R.E. Foreman, in addition to his mechanical duties, to see that suitable engines of the right class are available to work the rostered turns at the Depot, and it is the W.E. Foreman's responsibility to select suitable engines to work diagrammed or special turns at the Depot.

An extract from Harold Rudgard's 'Motive Power Organization and Practice', 1946, regarding Engine Diagrams. He was the LMS Superintendent of Motive Power at the time, having succeeded D. C. Urie three years earlier, and was known throughout the railway as 'The Colonel'.

ENGINE WORKINGS ONLY.

```
TURN 32        THREE CLASS 4F (STD. 0-6-0)
'A'
(AMENDED              Rowsley Nth. Jn.    3.14am    Bank      MO        (298)
7.11.60)              (3.5am Rowsley to Heaton Mersey)
  4. 9am              Peak Forest Nth.    4.15      LE        MO
  5.10                Shed                6.30      LE        MO
                      Rowsley Nth.Jn.     7. 4      Bank      MO
                      (6.55am to Chaddesden) Chadderton
  .8. 8               Peak Forest Sth.    8.28      LE        MO
  9.14                Rowsley Shed
                      Rowsley Nth.Jn.     5. 0      Bank      MX        (276)
                      (4.51am from Rowsley)
  6. 6                Buxton No. 1        7.25      LE Cpld   MX
  8.18                Rowsley Shed                                      MO    MX   Cancelled
                      Rowsley             12. 2pm   TF        D         (355)(331) 9F/234
  5.46pm              Walton              —         LE        D         (27B/190-191)
  5.56                Walton Shed
'B'
(Amended              Walton Up Sdgs.     1.20am    TF        MSX       (27E/128) )
 27.3.61)
  2.27am              Warrington C.       3.40      TF        MSX                  )
  5.10                Walton Dn. Sdgs.                                              )
                      Walton Sdgs.        8.30      Frt       SX                    ) TARGET
 11.18                Halewood            12.15pm   Frt       SX        (27E/129)   ) 120
 12.23pm              Allerton Depot                                                 )
                      SHUNT as required (Frt)                                        )
                      Allerton Depot      1.45      Frt       SX                    )
  1.54                Halewood Nth. Sdgs. 2.53      Frt       SX                    )
  3.18                Walton Sdgs.        3.23      LE        SX                    )
  3.28                Walton Shed
                      Walton Shed         7.13pm    LE        SX
                      Huskisson           8. 0      EF(D)     SX        (27E/126&116)(345)
 12.30am              Rowsley Sdgs.
                      Walton Sdgs.        7.20am    Eties     SO        (27E/103)(9F/240)
  1. 5pm              Rowsley Sdgs.
"C" portion unaltered
                      Rowsley Sidings     6.50am    TF        MSX       (389)
  8.40am              Chaddesden          10.25     Min       MSX
 10.44                Derby Shed          11.34     LE        MSX
 11.42                St. Marys           12.12pm   Min       MSX
  1.15pm              Rowsley Sdgs.
                      Rowsley Sth. Jn.    2.54pm    Bank      MSX       (287)
                      (1.25pm St. Marys to Shotwick Sdgs.)
  4.32                Peak Forest Nth.    5.14      LE        MWSX
  6.10                Rowsley Shed
                      Peak Forest North   4.55      LE        WO
  5. 3                Tunstead            5.55      Bank      WO
  6.12                Peak Forest         —         LE        WO
                      Rowsley Shed
                      Rowsley Nth.Jn.     1.40pm    Asst.     SO        (375)
  4.12pm              Cheadle Heath
                      Cheadle Sdgs.       5.25      Eties     SO
  7.27                Rowsley Sdgs.
                      Rowsley Nth.Jn.     11.59pm   Bank      SO        (307)
                      (11.50pm Rowsley to Cheadle V. Jn.)
  2.45am              Bibbington Sdgs.    3.10am    LE        Sun
  4.25                Rowsley Shed
```

Cyclical engine diagram No. 32 involving three of Rowsley's 4F 0-6-0s or 'Derby Fours' as they were dubbed. The figures in parenthesis referred to the associated Enginemen's Workings, both Rowsley and elsewhere including Aintree, Walton and Heaton Mersey.

Rowsley's 44101 passing Derby South Junction signal box in May 1959 with, possibly, the 6.50 Class H Rowsley–Chaddesden mentioned in Part C of the cyclical engine diagram, Turn 32 (q.v.).
R. J. BUCKLEY/
INITIAL PHOTOGRAPHICS

ENGINE AND MEN'S WORKINGS

ONE CLASS 3F TANK (MID. 0-6-0)
UP SIDINGS SHUNT

TARGET 66

TURN 150

			Book on a.m.	Book off p.m.	H.M.
	Shed	5.55am LE	5.10	1.10	8.0
6.0am	Rowsley Up Sdgs	SHUNT			
	RELIEF 12.50pm by Turn 151	MO			

TURN 151 TARGET 66

			p.m.	p.m.	
	RELIEVE Turn 150 at 12.50pm	MO	12.30	8.15	7.45
12.50pm	SHUNT	MO			
	Rowsley U Sdgs 8. 0pm LE	MO			
8. 5	Shed	MO			
	RELIEF on arrival	MO			

TURN 152 TARGET 66

			p.m.	p.m.	
	ENGINE PREPARED by Turn 440	SX	9.40	5.40	8.0
	Shed 9.55pm LE	SX			
10. 0pm	Rowsley U Sdgs	SX			
	SHUNT 5.20am	SX			
	RELIEF 5.20am by Turn 154	MX			

TURN 153 TARGET 66

			p.m.	a.m.	
	RELIEVE Turn 155 at 8. 0pm	SO	7.40	3.20	7.40
8. 0pm	SHUNT 11.30pm	SO			
11.30	RELIEF for meal 11.50 by Turn 306	SO			
11.50	SHUNT 2.30am	SO/Sun			
	Rowsley Up Sdgs 2.30	Sun			
2.35am	Shed				
	DISPOSE				

TURN 154 TARGET 66

			a.m.	p.m.	
	RELIEVE Turn 152 at 5.20am	MX	5. 0	1. 0	8.0
5.20am	SHUNT 12.40pm	MX			
	RELIEF 12.40pm by Turn 155	MX			

TURN 155 TARGET 66

			p.m.	p.m.	
	RELIEVE Turn 154 at 12.40pm	MX	12.20	8.15	7.55MSX
12.40pm	SHUNT 8. 0pm	MX	12.20	8.20	8. 0SO
	Rowsley U Sdgs 8. 0pm LE	MSX			
8. 5	Shed	MSX			
	RELIEF on arrival	MSX			
	RELIEF 8. 0pm by Turn 153	SO			

A pageful of diagrams referring to the one engine booked to the Up Sidings, South End, Shunt. Rowsley men called all shunting engines 'Jockos' irrespective of class, a Midland 0-6-0T, Standard 0-6-0T or even a spare J94 0-6-0ST off the C&HPR.

ENGINEMEN'S WORKINGS ONLY

TURN 278

			Book on a.m.	Book off p.m.	H.M.
	ENGINE PREPARED by Turn 437		10.10	3.37	5.27MSO
	Shed 11.10am LE		10.55	7.22	8.27MSX
	Rowsley North Jn 11.44 Bank	MSX			
	(11.36am from Rowsley)	D (16B/60)			
12.50pm	Buxton No.1 (11.12am from Mold Junction)				
	Rowsley Old Yard 5.42pm Eties	MSX			
6.47	RELIEF 6.47pm for Kirkby				
	by 16B Turn 210	MSO (16B/60)			
12.50	Buxton No.1 1.50pm LE	MSO			
2.42	Rowsley M.P.D.	MSO			
	DISPOSE				

TURN 341

			night	a.m.	
			12. 0	6.35	6.35
	Shed 12.45am LE	MX			
	Rowsley Sidings 1.10 EF(D)	MX	(27E/48)(27E/51)		
2.33am	Cheadle Sidings	MX			
	RELIEF 2.33am fro Walton	MX			
	by 27E Turn 116.				
	TAKE TO ENGINE PREPARED				
	by 9F Turn 417.				
	Heaton Mersey Shed 3.15am LE	MX	(16B/60)		
	Cheadle Sidings 3.45 Eties	MX			
5.35	Rowsley Sidings - LE	MX			
5.40	Shed				
	DISPOSE				

A couple of Enginemen's Workings Only diagrams in which the items in parenthesis are, this time, the associated engine diagrams, in these cases featuring Kirkby and Walton.

Mary's – Shotwick up to Peak Forest. The sundry Mondays only (MO), Saturdays only (SO), etc. variations can be easily determined with all the associated Enginemen's Only turns shown in parenthesis.

A whole pageful of Engine & Men's Workings, turns 150 to 155, as illustrated, cover Rowsley Up Sidings Target 66 with the usual adjustments for MO, MX, SO, Sun., but, basically, the engine is at work in the sidings from 8.0 Monday until 2.30 Sunday, with two-hourly visits to the shed for servicing each evening except Saturday.

A couple of accompanying Enginemen's Workings Only, turns 278 and 341, with the associated Engine Workings now in parenthesis, highlight, apart from anything else, that since the wartime reduction of lodging turns, Rowsley men did not go beyond Buxton onto the Western Division, or seldom beyond Cheadle on the Midland Division. Prior to that there had been lodging jobs to Garston, Longsight, Walton, Oldham and elsewhere. There were also reciprocal foreign turns into Rowsley although there was no railway hostel or 'barracks' as they were termed. The visiting crews lodged in houses such as at Mrs. Wardle's on Dale Road. One such visitor was Charlie Harrison from Oldham, Lees. He'd started life at the Buxton LNW shed as a caller-up in 1917, progressed to passed cleaner and was actually on duty when the Class B 4-cylinder compound 0–8–0 No. 134 blew up. He transferred to Lees as a registered fireman in 1922 and chose to come to Rowsley as a driver in 1940. There he became known as 'Wag', not least because of his championing of the Super D. "If they give me one each time I book on," he'd say, "they can scratch my name off the holiday list." A personal friend, he lived to nearly 97 and still maintained that there were "No bad'uns among Ds."

Many foreign engines came onto the shed, either with their own crews to turn, water and clean the fire ('Turnbacks' we called them) or as part of the Rowsley diagrams. Sometimes a stranger, properly termed an 'unbalanced engine', would arrive, however, and that is where another side of engine management came in. Every Running Foreman had an opposite number in the District Control Office, the Motive Power Controller, who was in touch with the Divisional Control Room. *Operating Control Organisation*, ERO

My Foreman's Assistant, Jack Greaves, known unaccountably as 'Clunch', posed beside the racks containing, at the bottom, Drivers' Repair Cards and spare Weekly Notices, and above, the diagram wallets ready for distribution. K. MILES

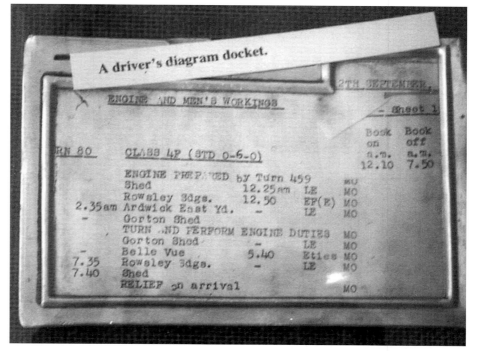

When signing on, drivers were issued with a copy of the relevant diagram encased in a metal frame with a Perspex window known as a 'wallet'. This example was photographed at a Rowsley Association exhibition and, as it happens, includes a rare visit to a former LNER shed. K. MILES

In the early 'fifties, Super Ds were regular visitors to the shed. One from Speke Junction, for example, worked in on the 8.0 Empties from Garston and returned with the 9/58 Mineral to Edge Hill. This one, however, 49451 of Patricroft, was definitely an unbalanced foreigner. K. MILES

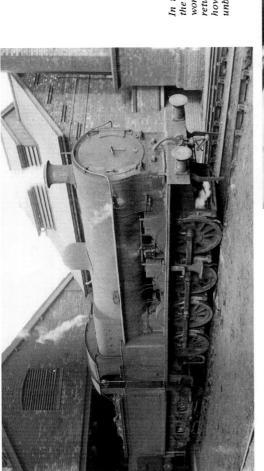

Charlie 'Wag' Harrison at a mere 91 aboard one of his beloved Super Ds, the preserved 9395, then at the Midland Railway Centre. He became involved with the Peak Rail preservation project and the approach road off the A6 at Rowsley South is named 'Harrison Way'.
F. MORTON/ROWSLEY ASSOCIATION

Yours truly at work in the Regional Motive Power Office, Euston, in 1955 still clad in my Running Foreman's blue duster coat. Two were issued annually plus a mackintosh every three years.
K. MILES

52457, made it quite clear that 'with regard to unbalanced foreign engines, this information must be given to the Control Room currently.' Further, that 'the regulation of unbalanced engines must be supervised very closely in the Control Room. It must be understood that the use of foreign engines on workings which are allocated to any Depot other than that to which it belongs, must be regarded as an arrangement only to be adopted in an emergency, and not to be resorted to without direct authority from the Divisional Control Office. Similarly, home engines must not be used on trains booked to be worked by foreign engines without consulting the Divisional Control Office.'

Incidentally, it must also be understood that once an engine left the depot, both it and its crew ceased to be a Motive Power responsibility and became totally under the supervision of the Operating Department through its Control Offices. So, in addition to reporting unbalanced engines currently, the Running Foreman had also to relay the engine number and crew signing-on times for each of the depot's workings. I had a good working relationship with my opposite number, Ron Cochran, who, although stationed at the Derby District Control Office, still lived in Darley Dale having previously worked in the old Rowsley Control Office until its closure in 1948. Over and above all the current exchange of information, every Running Foreman was required to 'advise the Control Room at 5.0 each day, the "Power Position" which must include information in regard to home engines away without booked or pre-arranged return workings, unbalanced foreign engines on hand, and foreign engines on hand under repair.' In addition, as and when such circumstances arose, 'The Control Room must be acquainted with the causes of late starts of engines from a Motive Power Depot, and prior advice must be given to the Control Room when it is anticipated that the booked gonging-off time is likely to be departed from.' Also, of course, in amongst all these exchanges, there were conversations regarding such as paths for engines to the shops or trial runs after repair, any change in engine class for a particular working, details of engines and crews for double heading or special workings, jobs for Control Relief sets, advice of any engines and/or enginemen becoming spare, and so on. All this while dealing with the vagaries of the enginemen booking on duty every few minutes ... a heady atmosphere and one in which, I confess, I revelled.

LMS TIMES

LMS JOURNAL No. 21

I know that it is trespassing on LNER territory, but to follow up the letter from Don Rowland, the actual date of abolition of carriage side lights on LNER trains was Monday, 5th May 1924, as this extract from Northern Scottish Area Weekly Circular No. 71 of 1st May 1924 includes the instruction 'Side and tail lamps on coaching stock — only one tail lamp required from 5.5.24 (M). WR23121'.

Keith Fenwick

There has not been any further comment from readers, so the question of when the LMS ceased to require side lamps on coaching stock remains unresolved and I cannot add anything else to the article that was published in LMSJ No. 19. *(Editor)*

I was very taken with the excellent photograph of 15103 on page 76 of Journal No. 21. This became the sole surviving example of Drummond's two-dozen engines of the 171 class built for light branch line work between 1884 and 1891. Only fifteen survived into the LMS, taking numbers 15100-15114, and all but 15103 were withdrawn between 1924 and 1930. This was withdrawn in November 1944 but lingered in the 'Dump' at St. Rollox until August 1946 when it went to Kilmarnock for breaking up. James Stevenson's photograph portrays it in May 1946 and keen eyes will spot that the building plate is missing. That, 'LMS Rebuilt 1924 St. Rollox' (it received a new boiler pressed to 160 psi with a steel firebox), and the tank plate 'Water Capacity 830 gallons', together with the shed plate, 32A, all came into my possession but were, sadly, given away.

The question raised regarding braking was also of interest, particularly in respect of one of the so-called Stanier 0–4–4Ts, 6408, which left Willesden for Edinburgh, Dalry Road, in October 1935. In correspondence, James Stevenson, who actually saw it running light past the shed on one occasion, suggested that the intention was perhaps to compare its performance with the Caley engines. Having no Westinghouse brake, however, it would seem that all it was fit for was empty carriage workings in and out of Princes Street with main line stock. Whatever the reason, it was back at Willesden the following April.

In the same issue in 'Time On!' on page 63: 'Five ... Four ... Three ... Two ... One ... *8 o'clock*'. Dear, oh dear! It would seem that Wild Swan's scanner was either still working on GMT or was unable to read my beautifully hand-printed 9! Finally, on the rear cover it reads 'for lager generations'. Is this a deliberate mistake?

Keith Miles
Seaton, Devon

Further to the excellent series of articles regarding the 'Lickey Incline, its Locomotives and Operation', I would like, if possible, to make some additional comments.

Page 57 — The Fowler 3F 0–6–0 Tanks. 47466 was listed in the text as being one of the Bromsgrove allocations for 1954. Personally, I never observed that particular engine working at Bromsgrove. It was at the time based in Liverpool. However, 47565 at that date had been a long-serving member of the stud of Bromsgrove bankers.

47276 and 47308, again both longtime Bromsgrove residents, remained in use until March 1964 and not 1961 as stated. This pair actually outlived two of the seven more modern WR 94XX 0–6–0PTs sent to Bromsgrove as replacements for the 'Jinties', surviving as they did until just a few months prior to closure of the shed. Even in the 1960s other 'Jinties' made brief appearances at Bromsgrove. For example, 47506, a Gloucester Barnwood engine, spent much of 1963 at the shed.

Saltley-based 47313, as is well known, was a regular performer at Bromsgrove throughout most of the 1950s. This engine, along with six others of the class, had been built by Bagnalls of Stafford in 1929 for the S&DJR as their number 22. It was absorbed, together with all S&DJR stock, into the LMS fold during 1930. After being transferred away from Bromsgrove, 47313 continued to soldier on, becoming one of half a dozen to survive into 1967. Although the 'Jinties' are well represented in preservation, it is unfortunate that 47313 was not selected due to its S&DJR lineage. It would be nice to see one of the preserved 'Jinties' turned out in S&DJR blue livery. What a fine sight it would make pounding up Lickey Bank and coupled to the S&D 7F 2–8–0 No. 88 with perhaps a BR 9F 2–10–0 at the rear. Wishful thinking!

The Hawksworth 94XX WR 0–6–0PTs — The Lickey Incline came under Western Region operational control during 1948. As a consequence, ex-GWR locomotives moved into the area. At that time the 94XX bankers were already well established at Bromsgrove. These were numbered in block 8400-6, the first arriving in the summer of 1956. The others followed during the next six months, but not in numerical order.

Other locomotives — For many years Bromsgrove always had a couple of ex-MR goods tender engines amongst the allocation. These were used for local freight trips and yard shunting. On rare occasions they could be observed on banking duties, pressed into service during the busy July/August holiday periods. When required, they did not bank solo but always in tandem. Ex-MR 3F 43762 comes to mind performing this duty.

Other interesting types have included 0–4–0 tanks. Ex-CR 'Pug' 56020 arrived from Burton in 1952. It was little used and probably served as a stationary boiler. When it was hauled away dead in 1955, it was replaced by another 'Pug' for a short duration, being ex-L&Y 51217.

Continued on page 80

The Kettering to Huntingdon Line
by STANLEY C. JENKINS, MA

RUNNING for the little less than 48 miles across the counties of Northamptonshire, Huntingdonshire and Cambridgeshire, the cross-country route from Kettering to Cambridge was, in its heyday, a useful freight and passenger link serving a wide rural area. The line was in effect two routes placed end-to-end, the eastern section between Cambridge and St Ives being a former Eastern Counties branch, while the western portion from Kettering to Huntingdon became part of the Midland Railway; the short intervening section of line between Huntingdon and St Ives eventually passed into joint GER and Great Northern control. This present study will concentrate on the Midland end of the route.

ORIGINS OF THE LINE
The Eastern Counties branch from Chesterton Junction, near Cambridge, to St Ives, originated during the Railway Mania years of the middle 1840s when the ECR promoted a line which, in connection with the Ely & Huntingdon Railway, would form a through route between Cambridge and Huntingdon. If successfully implemented, this scheme would also have provided a connection with a proposed Midland Railway branch at Huntingdon which, in turn, would have provided connections to a whole range of destinations in the south and east Midlands via a suggested 'South Midlands Railway'.

In the event, the South Midlands scheme was not immediately successful, and when opened to public traffic on 17th August 1847, the ECR branch from Cambridge was of purely local importance. At St Ives, the Eastern Counties line formed a junction with the Ely & Huntingdon section of the East Anglian Railways, which was opened on the same day as the ECR route. The new line thereby formed part of a link between Cambridge and Huntingdon, but in practice St Ives soon became the western terminus of the branch, and there was only a limited service on the four and a half mile section between St Ives and Huntingdon (Godmanchester). At one stage, this short EAR line was worked by horse traction!

Initial attempts to create a useful cross-country route between Cambridge, Huntingdon and Kettering were thereby negated, although the obvious advantages of such a link from the south Midlands to East Anglia continued to exercise the minds of ambitious railway promoters. In the meantime, the Eastern Counties Railway was able to consolidate its hold on the lines in and around Cambridge, and in 1852 the ECR managed to secure control of the East Anglian Railways, including the short branch to Huntingdon; ten years later both companies became part of the newly-created Great Eastern Railway when that company was formed in 1862.

In the west, the Midland Railway had also become well-established as a major company, and this led to inevitable demands that the missing link between the MR at Kettering and the ECR at Huntingdon might be filled by an independent company which would, however, be supported by one or other of the two main-line companies. Accordingly, in 1861, the Kettering & Thrapstone Railway was formed as a means of securing the hoped-for rail link between the manufacturing districts of the Midlands and the ports on the East Anglian coast.

Ex-MR 2–4–0 No. 20225 at speed near Thrapston on 14th April 1936 with a three-coach Ordinary passenger train. The Islip Iron Company's system can be seen to the north of the main line.
H. F. WHEELLER

The Kettering & Thrapstone prospectus pointed out that the proposed line would connect the Midland Railway at Kettering with the Great Northern main line at Huntingdon, and, in addition to serving the needs of a large agricultural district, the new railway would enable coal, lime and manufactured goods to be brought into the area at greatly reduced cost. It was also pointed out that the surrounding area was rich in iron ore, which could not be fully exploited until transport facilities had been improved by the provision of a rail link.

Supporters of the scheme included prominent local landowners such as Lord Overton of Overton Hall, the Duke of Buccleuch of Boughton House near Kettering, and the Duke of Manchester, who resided on the route of the proposed railway at Kimbolton.

With solid local support, and the backing of the main-line railway companies, the Bill for 'Making a Railway between Kettering and Thrapstone' was sent up to Parliament in the 1862 session. After an easy passage, the scheme received the Royal Assent on 29th July 1862.

The resulting Act (25 & 26 Vic.cap.173) provided consent for a railway commencing 'in the parish of Kettering in the County of Northampton by a junction with the Leicester and Hitchin Railway of the Midland Railway Company' and terminating 'in the parish of Thrapstone in the County of Northampton, in a field abutting the west side of the Northampton and Peterborough Railway of the London & North Western Railway Company'. Capital of £80,000 in ten pound shares was authorised, together with a further £26,000 by loan. The number of directors was fixed at five, the qualification for board membership being £300.

Having obtained their Act of Incorporation, the supporters of the Kettering & Thrapstone Railway were keen to begin construction, but at the same time it was agreed that a further Parliamentary Bill should be lodged in the 1863 session in order that the company could secure consent for an eastwards continuation of the authorised line from Kettering. This second Bill passed successfully through every stage of the complex Parliamentary process, and on 28th July 1863 the Act authorising 'the Kettering & Thrapstone Railway Company to extend their authorised line of Railway to Huntingdon, with a Branch Railway at Huntingdon' received the Royal Assent.

The second Act (26 & 27 Vic.cap.203) provided consent for an eighteen-mile extension of the Kettering & Thrapstone route which would run south-eastwards from Thrapstone for around five miles and thence east towards Huntingdon, where the line would pass beneath the Great Northern Railway and effect a junction with the Great Eastern system; a short branch would provide a useful link with the GNR line.

The line would be worked by the Midland Railway, and, by agreement with the GER, the Midland company would have Powers for running through trains over the Kettering and Huntingdon line from Sheffield, Nottingham, Derby, Leicester and other places to Cambridge. The Act permitted the Kettering & Thrapstone company to install three public level crossings at Longstow, Easton and Grafham, subject to the provision of gate lodges staffed by gate keepers who would ensure the safety of the public.

In engineering terms, the authorised route from Kettering presented very few problems. Leaving the Midland main line at Kettering Junction, the route would cross the River Ise and then surmount a ridge of higher land before descending eastwards towards the Nene Valley. A further climb would be required on the east side of the valley, beyond which the proposed line would traverse easy terrain as it approached Huntingdon.

Messrs Waring Brothers were awarded the main contract for construction of the line and, with George Bruce as Engineer, rapid progress was made. The major earthworks were substantially complete by the Autumn of 1864, and at the half-year meeting held in February 1865 it was reported that over two miles of trackwork had been laid, while the station buildings were being proceeded with.

In an atmosphere of increasing optimism it was confidently predicted that the railway would be opened for public traffic by the summer of 1865. In reality, this hope could not be realised, and numerous minor problems were identified when the line was examined by Captain F. H. Rich, RE, the Board of Trade Inspector. Captain Rich refused to pass the line for public traffic until these problems had been rectified, and a second BOT inspection was necessary in February 1866. On this occasion the Inspecting Officer was satisfied that progress had been made, and the line was therefore opened for goods traffic on 21st February and for the carriage of passengers on 1st March 1866.

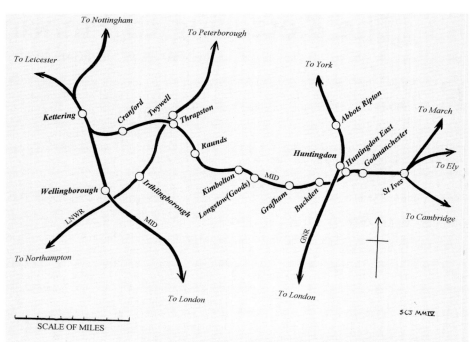

Sketch of the Kettering to Huntingdon line and other railways.

The Opening Day was a comparatively low-key affair, although large numbers of local people turned out to see the first trains pass along the new railway. The line was single track throughout, with intermediate stations at Cranford, Twywell, Thrapstone, Raunds, Kimbolton, Grafham and Brampton. The principal engineering features were the river bridges across the Nene at Thrapstone and over the Ouse at Huntingdon. Elsewhere, there were numerous over or underbridges, together with several cuttings and embankments.

The stations were attractively built in local building materials, those on the western section of the route being of stone construction with stone roofing slates, which blended perfectly with the surrounding farms and villages. All train services were operated by the Midland Railway, which had agreed to work the Kettering to Huntingdon line in return for 40 per cent of the gross receipts for an initial period of seven years, and thereafter for 50 per cent in perpetuity.

SUBSEQUENT HISTORY

The line was, from its inception, a relatively busy freight route which carried lucrative iron ore in addition to the usual types of freight traffic such as coal, agricultural produce and building materials. Iron ore workings were established at various places *en route*, and by the 1880s there were rail-connected excavations at or near Cranford, Twywell, Thrapstone and Raunds. The workings at Raunds were short-lived, though iron ore extraction continued to develop on a very extensive scale between Kettering and Thrapston.

Significant changes took place at the eastern end of the Kettering to Huntingdon line during the early 1880s, when a new through station was opened for passenger traffic at Huntingdon East. This was in effect a joint station used by three companies, the former East Anglian Railways line between Huntingdon and St Ives having by that time become part of the Great Northern & Great Eastern Joint Railway.

The new station was laid out in such a way that GN&GE services could make use of the two centre tracks, whereas Midland trains to and from the Kettering line could use only the outer face of an island platform during the normal course of operations.

The Kettering, Thrapston & Huntingdon Railway remained nominally independent for over thirty years, but finally, in 1897, the local company was absorbed by the Midland Railway. As such, the Kettering to Huntingdon line passed into LMS ownership on 1st January 1923 under the provisions of the Railways Act 1921.

There had, by that time, been several further changes; for example, the line from Kettering Junction to Huntingdon had been fully re-signalled in accordance with MR practice, standard Midland Railway hip-roofed signal cabins being provided at the various stations and sidings *en route* to Huntingdon East. Most of these boxes dated from the 1890s and, as such, they were of the familiar Midland type with half-height windows at the sides and much deeper 12-pane window frames at the front.

Other relatively minor changes included the re-naming of Thrapstone and Brampton stations, Thrapstone having been changed to Thrapston in 1885, while Brampton became Buckden station with effect from 1st February 1868.

The line became particularly busy during World War Two when there was exceptional demand for British iron ore in connection with the war effort. With petrol rationing in force and the railways under government control for the duration of the war, freight and passenger traffic was sent by rail in preference to road transport, and this ensured that the railway system played a major role in the 1939–45 conflict. As the war effort got into full stride, a huge programme of aerodrome construction was put into effect, and in this context the Kettering to Huntingdon route began to carry large quantities of building materials.

Three airfields were built in the immediate vicinity, one of these being at Kimbolton while the other two were at Molesworth and Chelveston. Kimbolton aerodrome was situated immediately to the south of the railway near Kimbolton station, whilst Molesworth was four miles to the north. The third airfield, at Chelveston, was a little over three miles to the south-west of Raunds station. Each of these aerodromes covered approximately two square miles, and their buildings, runways and dispersal areas required around 640,000 square yards of concrete in each case, together with various other supplies and constructional materials.

Most of the materials needed for the new aerodromes was brought into the area by rail, and, to facilitate this new traffic flow, extra sidings were installed at Kimbolton station and at nearby Long Stow.

Once the airfields were completed, they received their aircraft allocations which, in this case, were B-17 Flying Fortresses operated by the 8th United States Army Air Force. By 1943, Kimbolton and Molesworth were both being used by part of the 103rd Provisional Combat Bombardment Wing, Colonel Maurice Preston's 379th Group being stationed at Kimbolton, while Colonel Kermit D. Steven's 303rd Group ('The Hell's Angels') flew from Molesworth.

Kimbolton and the other local aerodromes were supplied by rail, with fuel and ammunition being delivered regularly by train. In this context it is perhaps worth mentioning that a 500 bomber raid on occupied Europe would require no less than 80 tank wagons of aviation fuel, together with 300 tons of equipment and around 7,500 tons of spare parts in immediate readiness. In the case of the Kettering to Huntingdon route, the supply trains needed to supply the US 8th Army Air Force had to travel over a single line that was also being heavily used for the movement of vital iron ore, while all of this activity would of course have been carried out under wartime conditions, with nightly blackouts enforced.

LOCOMOTIVES & TRAIN SERVICES IN THE MIDLAND & LMS ERAS

The first timetable provided just four trains each way between Kettering and Cambridge on weekdays and two up and two down workings on Sundays. In the eastbound direction, up trains left Kettering at 8.15 am, 11.30 am, 2.50 pm and 6.30 pm, whilst down services left Cambridge at 7.45 am, 11.05 am, 3.00 pm and 6.15 pm. On Sundays, the frequency was reduced to two trains in each direction, with

Former Midland 2-4-0 No. 20012 pulling away from the single-platform station at Cranford with a down passenger working from Cambridge to Kettering in 1937; this locomotive was built in 1867.
T. G. HEPBURN

KETTERING TO CAMBRIDGE
July 7th to September 21st 1930 Working Time Table of Freight Trains

UP LINE

Most of the trains were classified as Mineral, but where other train classifications applied these are shown. All trains departed from Kettering, at the times as below.
Times are shown as 0.00 = a.m. 0/00 = p.m.
Most trains were booked to take water at Thrapston.

Monday Excepted	Depart from Kettering	2.10 arrive Cranford Sidings East 2.42
Monday Excepted	ditto	4.45 arrive Cambridge 8.0
Monday Only	ditto	4.35 arrive Cambridge 10.10
Monday Excepted	ditto	5.10 arrive Kimbolton 6.40
Monday Only	ditto	5.40 arrive Cambridge 10.0
Monday Excepted	ditto	5.40 arrive Kimbolton 7.5
Daily	ditto	9.40 arrive Kimbolton 10.40
	ditto	10.12 arrive Cambridge 2/40
Stopping Freight	ditto	10.40 arrive Thrapston 11.57
Stopping Freight	ditto	12/5 arrive Godmanchester 3/10
	ditto	2/32 arrive Kimbolton 3/24
	ditto	2/45 arrive Cambridge 5/38
	ditto	3/10 arrive Thrapston 4/33
	ditto	6/5 arrive Cambridge 9/0
Saturday Only	ditto	8/35 arrive Kimbolton 9/35
Saturday Excepted Engine and Brake	ditto	8/35 arrive Twywell, Youngs Sidings 9/5
Saturday Excepted	ditto	9/25 arrive Kimbolton 10/35

Sunday

There was only one Up train on a Sunday. This was classified as Empties, which departed from Kettering at 12.15 and arrived at Thrapston at 1.35 after spending fifteen minutes at Youngs Siding.

DOWN LINE

Most of the trains were classified as Mineral, but those that were not are shown.

Monday Excepted	3.5 from Cranford Sidings East to Kettering arrive 3.28
Daily	7.5 from Kimbolton as Engine and Brake to Islip thence Mineral to Kettering arrive 8.23
Monday Excepted	9.40 from Cambridge arrive Kettering 2/40
Daily	11.17 Engine and Brake from Kimbolton arrive Kettering 12/46
Daily	1/10 from Thrapston arrive Kettering 2/4
Daily	4/5 from Kimbolton as Engine and Brake to Youngs Sidings thence Mineral arrive Kettering 5/15
Daily	1/42 from Cambridge arrive Kettering 7/12
Daily	4/55 Stopping Freight from Godmanchester arrive Kettering 7/53
Daily	7/20 from Thrapston arrive Kettering 8/6
Daily	4/35 Empties from Cambridge arrive Kettering 9/8
Saturday Excepted	9/20 from Youngs Siding arrive Kettering 9/58
Daily	7/45 from Cambridge arrive Kettering 10/40
Saturday Only	10/10 from Kimbolton arrive Kettering 11/44
Saturday Excepted	10/55 from Kimbolton arrive Kettering 12.42
Saturday Only	10/10 from Cambridge arrive Kettering 12.52
Saturday Excepted	10/0 from Cambridge arrive Kettering 12.58

Sunday

The only Sunday train was the return working of the Empties from Kettering to Thrapston. The train ran as Engine and Brake from Thrapston at 2.0 arrive Kettering 3.0.

up services from Kettering at 9.45 am and 7.30 pm, and corresponding down workings from Cambridge at 6.45 am and 4.25 pm.

The original train service, with its basic pattern of four up and four down workings between Kettering, Huntingdon and Cambridge, persisted for many years, with minor variations in the times of arrival or departure. There were in general two morning trains and two afternoon services, which accomplished the 48 mile through journey in about two hours. In the 1880s, eastbound workings departed from Kettering at 8.25 am, 10.57 am, 3.30 pm and 7.10 pm, whilst balancing westbound services left Cambridge at 7.50 am, 11.30 am, 2.15 pm and 5.40 pm. There were, by that time, no longer any regular Sunday services.

In 1947, at the very end of the LMS period, local travellers were offered a choice of just three trains each way. In the up direction, trains departed from Kettering at 8.33 am, 2.10 pm and 5.20 pm, arriving at Cambridge at 10.15 am, 3.47 pm and 7.15 pm respectively; on Saturdays, the 5.20 pm working was replaced by a later train that left Kettering at 8.05 pm and reached Cambridge by 9.52 pm. The balancing down services departed from Cambridge at 7.30 am, 11.25 am and 4.55 pm, and arrived in Kettering at 9.13 am, 1.06 pm and 6.29 pm.

When opened in 1866, the Kettering, Thrapstone & Huntingdon Railway had probably been worked by former main-line locomotives. The Midland Railway was dominated by Nonconformist interests, and this may have engendered a parsimonious attitude towards outmoded locomotives that were kept in service so long as work could be found for them. Thus, in the 1860s, veteran 'Jenny Linds' and 'Sharpies' were still in service, whilst in later years the company's 2-4-0s and 0-6-0s enjoyed lives of remarkable longevity on rural backwaters such as the Huntingdon route.

The lengthy journey between Kettering and Cambridge meant that, in the 1930s, the line was typically worked by Kirtley or Johnson tender engines such as 2-4-0 No. 221 and Johnson Class 2F 0-6-0 No. 3545 which were both noted at Buckden by R. W. Kidner on 29th June 1933. In September 1934, *The Railway Magazine* reported that Kirtley 2-4-0 No. 20012 (formerly MR No. 12) was still in service. This veteran locomotive, built in 1867, was stationed at Kettering, and had 'frequently worked between there and Cambridge'. Although officially in store at Kettering, it was expected that 'this old engine' was 'likely to be in traffic again at any moment'.

Photographic evidence reveals that Midland 0-6-0s were employed on both passenger and goods workings, two further examples used on the route during the 1930s being Johnson Class 2F 0-6-0 No. 3195, and Class 3F 0-6-0 No. 3435. The usual passenger formation during the LMS era was three or four bogie vehicles, elliptical-roofed and clerestory stock being used apparently at random.

The heavy iron ore trains, which brought much activity to the western part of the line, were usually hauled by Midland 0–6–0s, though in later years the introduction of more powerful locomotives brought greater variety in the form of Stanier Class 5 4–6–0s and Class 8F 2–8–0s. The line was also used, to some extent, as a diversionary route during repairs or emergencies elsewhere on the system, though it would probably be true to say that the Kettering to Huntingdon line never really developed as a cross-country line. In fact, it remained very much a rural branch line which relied mainly on iron ore traffic for its principal source of revenue.

THE ROUTE AND STATIONS

Having examined the origins and history of the line from its inception until the LMS period, it would now be appropriate to consider the stations and route from Kettering to Huntingdon in greater detail, and the following section will therefore take readers on an imaginary guided tour of the line. The topographical details which follow will be correct for the later periods from the 1930s until closure in 1959, and the datum point for the calculation of distances will be Kettering Junction, some two miles to the south of Kettering station.

The Midland Railway reached Kettering on 8th May 1857, when the Leicester Bedford & Hitchin line was opened for public traffic as part of a tenuous through route to London King's Cross via Hitchin and the Great Northern main line. This original MR route to London remained in operation until the opening of the London extension between Bedford and St Pancras in 1868, after which the Midland Railway could claim that it had finally reached maturity as a great trunk route between London, the Midlands and the North of England.

Like other stations on the Leicester to Bedford line, Kettering had started life as a relatively unimportant wayside station on the Hitchin route to London, but subsequent traffic growth after the opening of the St Pancras extension ensured that the original facilities were progressively enlarged. The original station buildings could be seen on the up side of the line, though the most attractive features at this interesting Midland station were its extensive glass and iron canopies.

The line through Kettering was, like most of the Midland main line, increased to four tracks during the late Victorian period, with separate up and down lines for fast and slow traffic. The quadrupling was completed between 1889 and 1895, the four tracks being continued as far as Glendon, a little under 75 miles from London.

The layout at Kettering provided four platform faces, the centre platform being an island with tracks on both sides. The platforms were numbered from 1 to 5, the centre island comprising platforms 3 and 4. This platform was equipped with wooden buildings and further ridge-and-furrow canopies, while a further example of Midland Railway canopy construction could be seen on platform 5. These structures incorporated two distinct periods of construction, the original station building and canopy having been designed by C. Biddle during the 1850s, whilst various additions were made when the station was reconstructed during the 1890s.

There were three signal cabins in the vicinity of Kettering station, the main station box being sited between the fast and slow lines to the south of the platforms. Kettering North Box was on the up side, just two chains further north, while Kettering South Box was sited on the down side, to the south of the station. The station was able to handle all types of goods traffic including coal, livestock, vehicles, furniture and general merchandise; a large, red-brick goods shed was sited immediately to the east of the passenger station, and a 10-ton yard crane was able to deal with large or bulky consignments.

Johnson Class 2 0–6–0 No. 3127, photographed at Kettering on 27th March 1937, with a three-coach branch train. This locomotive was one of the Class 2 0–6–0s with 5ft 3in wheels.
H. F. WHEELLER

Kettering station, looking north towards Leicester on 25th April 1954, with platform 2 on the right, and the island platforms 3 and 4 to the left.   **COLLECTION R. J. ESSERY**

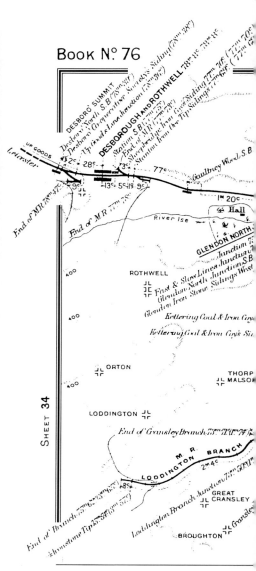

Kettering was a relatively complex station and, in addition to its role as the junction for branch services to Huntingdon and Cambridge, it also served as the junction for a short mineral line known as the Loddington Branch. The last-mentioned line diverged westwards on the down side of the running lines, and extended for 3 miles 65 chains serving, en route, the Cransley Iron & Steel Company's works and the Loddington Iron Company. For locomotive enthusiasts, the most interesting feature of Kettering station was probably the small, but busy motive power depot, which could be seen alongside the slow lines on the east side of the platforms.

Kettering Shed was a four-road structure with a double-gabled roof. It contained the usual coaling and watering facilities, together with a 60ft diameter locomotive turntable that had been installed by the LMS in 1938 to facilitate the introduction of Stanier Class 5MT 4-6-0s and other large engines. In early British Railways days the shed housed an assortment of around 38 locomotives, including Compound 4-4-0s Nos. 41012, 41053, 41063 and 41087, Ivatt Class 2MT 2-6-0s, Class 2F 0-6-0s and Class 4F 0-6-0s such as Nos. 43889, 43898, 44043, 44278 and 44465.

There was, in addition, a large allocation of Stanier Class 8F 2-8-0s for hauling the heavy ironstone trains that were so much a feature of the local railway scene. Some typical examples, during the BR period, included Nos. 48069, 48124, 49141, 48143, 48285, 48301, 48355, 48356, 48611, 48645, 48704 and 48759. These sturdy ex-LMS locomotives were subsequently joined by a number of British Railways Standard Class 9F 2-10-0s, which were ideally suited for hauling trains of iron ore. In 1959, the local allocation included 9F locomotives Nos. 92105, 92106, 92160, 92163 and 92164.

Leaving Kettering, Huntingdon trains headed southwards along the Midland main line to Kettering Junction, where the former Kettering, Thrapstone & Huntingdon Railway diverged eastwards from the Slow Goods lines. Perhaps surprisingly, the junction was controlled from what appeared at first glance to have been a London & North Western-style gabled signal cabin. In reality, the box was of LMS origin, and it had replaced an earlier Midland Railway cabin in 1935. The box featured a brick locking room and an external toilet at the top of the stairs; a separate stairway was also provided in connection with a small platform, from which the signalman was able to effect tablet exchanges.

The junction was, for many years, known officially as 'Cambridge Line Junction', although the attendant signal cabin was (apparently) always known as Kettering Junction Box. On 18th February 1906 a separate cabin, known as Pytchley Signal Box, was opened at the commencement of the first single-line section, just 30 chains from Cambridge Line Junction. However, this cabin had a comparatively short life and it was closed in 1935, its functions being taken over by the above-mentioned LMS box.

Shortly after diverging from the main line, the branch crossed the River Ise on a small bridge, after which the single track began to climb at 1 in 70. Entering a cutting, the line passed beneath three road overbridges in less than two miles and, heading more or less due east, reached Butlin's Siding signal box (2 miles 9 chains), which had formerly controlled a siding connection to ironstone workings at nearby Burton Latimer. The signal box, with 24 levers, was opened on 26th July 1906 and it remained in use long after quarrying ceased in the 1920s, Butlin's Sidings being used thereafter for occasional rolling stock storage.

Cranford, the first stopping place, was situated about one mile further on at 3 miles 27 chains. The facilities provided here consisted of a single platform on the up side of the running line, with a small goods yard immediately to the east. The layout incorporated a loop siding with connections at each end, together with two dead-end goods sidings which extended westwards towards the passenger station. There was a typical Midland hip-roofed signal cabin at the east end of the platform, and the goods yard contained the usual coal wharves, loading docks and cattle pens. The signal cabin, which dated from February 1892, was not a block post.

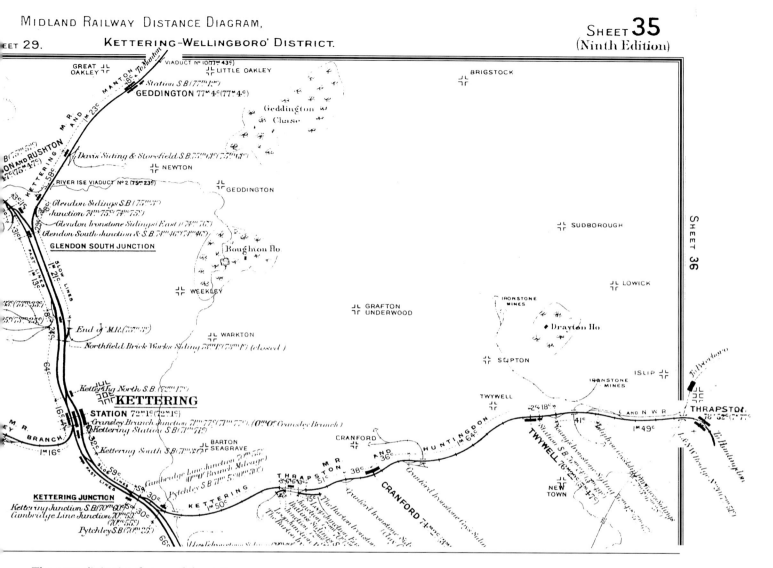

The most distinctive feature of the station was perhaps its ornate station building which, like others on the Kettering & Huntingdon line, was a building of considerable architectural pretention. The main block was a single-storey, stone-built structure with a gabled roof, but this essentially simple building was enlivened by the provision of a prominent two-storey gabled cross wing which provided domestic accommodation for the station master and his family; a hip-roofed extension projected from the west end of the building, and there was a rustic loggia on the east side of the cross wing. Other details included a projecting bay window and 'Tudor'-style mullioned windows.

Sadly, Cranford became a relatively early victim of rationalisation, its passenger services being withdrawn with effect from 2nd April 1956, although goods traffic continued to be handled until November 1961. The last scheduled passenger trains called on Saturday 31st March 1956.

A general view of Cranford station, looking east towards Huntingdon, and showing the stone station buildings. Cranford was not a block post or a staff station, its Midland signal box being merely a lever cabin.
LENS OF SUTTON

Twywell station, looking westwards from the road overbridge c.1930. The standard MR box was opened on 3rd February 1892 as a replacement for an earlier cabin.
COLLECTION R. J. ESSERY

There were extensive ironstone workings in the vicinity of the station, a fleet of 0–4–0ST and 0–6–0ST locomotives being employed by the Cranford Ironstone Company on a private quarry system that extended on both sides of the running lines. One of the industrial locomotives used on the ironstone company's line was *Sir Berkeley*, an 1890 Manning Wardle 0–6–0ST (Works No. 1210) that had been employed during the construction of the Great Central London extension and the GWR Westbury and Frome Cut-Off lines before its sale to the Cranford Ironstone Company in 1935.

Leaving Cranford, Huntingdon trains passed beneath a skew bridge carrying the A604 road across the line, and with evidence of ironstone extraction evident on all sides, the route dropped towards the Nene Valley. Twywell, the next stopping place, was another single-platform station, some 5 miles 47 chains from Kettering Junction. It consisted of a passenger platform and one dead-end goods siding trailing from the up direction on the south side of the running line.

The station building appeared, at first glance, to have been in the same architectural 'family' as that at Cranford, although in reality any similarities were purely superficial. As at Cranford, the building incorporated a two-storey station master's house with its gable end facing towards the platform, but in this case the building material was brick. This prominent domestic wing was flanked by an accretion of smaller extensions – the two-storey wing at the west end having a distinctive half-hipped gable. The windows were square-headed with bold lintels, and a tall brick chimney stack rose above the gabled roof.

The A604 road crossed the line on an overbridge at the east end of the platform, and there was a standard Midland hipped-roof signal cabin on the down side of the line between the platform ramp and the bridge. An array of ironstone sidings was provided on the east side of the overbridge to serve the needs of the Cargo Fleet Iron Company. The signal cabin, which was of the usual Midland hip-roofed design, had been opened on 3rd February 1892 to replace an earlier cabin. Like neighbouring Cranford, Twywell succumbed to rationalisation during the early BR period, its passenger and freight services being withdrawn with effect from 30th July 1951.

Continuing eastwards, trains soon reached further ironstone workings, which were served by a large network of 3ft gauge and standard-gauge lines belonging to Stewarts & Lloyds. There were interchange sidings on the up side of the Midland line, together with a lengthy loop line which was, until 1906, controlled from two MR boxes known as Islip Sidings West and Islip Sidings East, the Islip Iron Company being the original owner of the neighbouring ironstone works. An extension from the eastern end of the loop continued eastwards for about one mile in order to provide a tenuous connection with the nearby LNWR line (which also served the Islip Iron Works via a private siding connection).

The ironworks extended northwards for a considerable distance beyond the Midland route, and there was a three-mile 'main line' that continued past the villages of Islip and Lowick to quarries at Sudborough. It is interesting to discover that, during World War Two, Stewarts & Lloyds had considered the construction of a new mineral line between Islip mines and their main steelworks at nearby Corby. Hitherto, ore had been transported from Tywell to Corby via Kettering and the

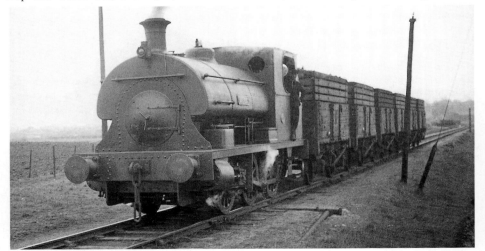

Islip Iron Company Peckett 0–6–0ST, photographed near Thrapston on 14th April 1936; Margot was built in 1918 (Works No. 1456).
H. F. WHEELLER

LMS, but the construction of about six miles of privately-owned line would have resulted in a much shorter route between the two Stewarts & Lloyds sites.

The wartime government was in favour of this new scheme, and planning reached an advanced stage. Indeed, Stewarts & Lloyds even ordered eight new 0–6–0STs from the Hunslet Engine Company, the first of which (Works No. 2411) was delivered to Corby in 1941. In the event, the proposed iron ore line was not built, though the Hunslet Engine order was completed, the seven remaining locomotives being sent to the War Department or other operators. On a footnote of history, the new 0–6–0STs were so successful that they became the prototypes for the famous 'Austerity' class saddle tanks that remained in production until 1961.

Having passed the Islip Iron Works, the MR branch climbed a 1 in 130 rising gradient which enabled it to cross the LNWR Northampton to Peterborough line on a girder bridge; beyond, the Midland line was carried across the River Nene on a nine-arch brick viaduct, after which another girder bridge spanned the A605 road as trains neared the principal intermediate station at Thrapston (Midland Road).

Situated 7 miles 77 chains from Kettering Junction, Thrapston was a two-platform station with slightly staggered up and down platforms on each side of a long crossing loop. The main station building was on the up side, and there was a small waiting shelter on the down platform. Water cranes were provided on both platforms, and there was a fully-equipped goods yard on the up side. The yard was entered by means of a trailing connection from the up running line.

The station building was another attractive, stone-built structure with Tudor gothic details. The building was arranged on the 'hall and cross wings' plan with two gabled wings linked by a longitudinal booking-hall block, one of the two cross wings being a two-storey structure while the other was of just one storey. The centre portion had an open-fronted loggia or waiting area with three gothic arches, and the single-storey cross wing was graced by a large bay window; the station master's domestic accommodation was located in the two-storey wing at the south end of the structure, while the booking office and waiting room accommodation was at the north end.

The goods yard contained coal wharves, a goods shed, cattle pens, loading facilities and a five-ton fixed yard crane. In operational terms, Thrapston was significant in that it marked the eastern limit of single-line tablet operation, the single-line sections beyond being worked by Train Staff in conjuction with block telegraph. This mode of operation had first been introduced in 1877–78, prior to which the entire branch had been worked by Train Staff. The station was controlled from a standard MR hip-roofed signal cabin that was sited to the east of the platforms on the up side, and had been opened on 3rd February 1892.

The station was originally referred to as Thrapstone, but the final 'e' was dropped at an early date and, thereafter, the spelling became simply Thrapston. In LMS days, the station was designated Thrapstone Midland Road to distinguish it from the nearby London & North Western station, which was known as Thrapston Bridge Street.

The station name was displayed in full on characteristic LMS 'Hawkseye' nameboards, which were made from minute spheres of reflective glass by the Birmingham-based firm of G. C. Hawkes. The signs, which were installed by the LMS from 1938 onwards as part of the company's 'brighter station' campaign, were originally yellow with black letters, though most were painted maroon and cream during the British Railways period, with cream letters on a dark red background.

From Thrapston, the railway proceeded south-eastwards on a 1 in 80 rising gradient and, after passing beneath three overbridges which carried minor lanes or farm tracks across

Thrapston station, looking south-east towards Huntingdon on 18th July 1958. The ornate station buildings were of stone construction. Note the barrow crossing between the two platforms.
H. C. CASSERLEY

Thrapston signal box was an utterly typical Midland Railway cabin, dating from 3rd February 1892. Cabins of this type were erected all over the MR system from around 1883 until c.1900; they have latterly become known as 'Type 2' cabins under the Signalling Record Society classification.
LENS OF SUTTON

the railway, trains approached the next station at Raunds, which was 11 miles 63 chains from Kettering Junction. Having passed under a further overbridge, eastbound workings came to rest in another small, single-platform station, with picturesque stone buildings and a small goods yard on the down side of the line.

The station building was in effect a mirror image of that at Cranford, both buildings being single-storey structures with a centrally-placed two-storey cross wing containing domestic accommodation for the station master and his family. At Raunds, however, the bay window that faced onto the platform was sited to the right of the central block, while the waiting room was to the left.

The goods yard was provided with two loop sidings and two dead-end roads; the yard entrance was trailing to up trains proceeding eastwards in the direction of Huntingdon but the loop siding also had a trailing connection from the down direction. One of the sidings served a covered goods shed, and there were also cattle pens and a loading dock. The station was signalled from another standard Midland hip-roofed timber cabin on the up side of the running lines. This characteristic MR structure had been opened on 29th July 1891.

Departing from Raunds, trains continued south-eastwards for a little over one mile, after which the line curved leftwards onto an easterly heading as it crossed the county boundary between Northamptonshire and Huntingdonshire. Passing beneath a succession of minor overbridges, eastbound workings soon reached Kimbolton (16 miles 11 chains), where a surprisingly large station was provided – a reflection, perhaps, of the proximity of Kimbolton Castle, the ancestral seat of the Dukes of Manchester.

Kimbolton was a crossing station with up and down platforms, its main station building and goods yard being on the down side. The yard, which incorporated three sidings, had trailing connections from both up and down directions. It was provided with a brick goods shed whilst a further siding trailed from the up side. In World War Two, four Air Ministry sidings were installed on the east side of the overbridge which crossed the line at the Huntingdon end of the platforms. The 1938 Railway Clearing House *Handbook of Stations* reveals that Kimbolton was fully-equipped with a full range of accommodation for coal, live-

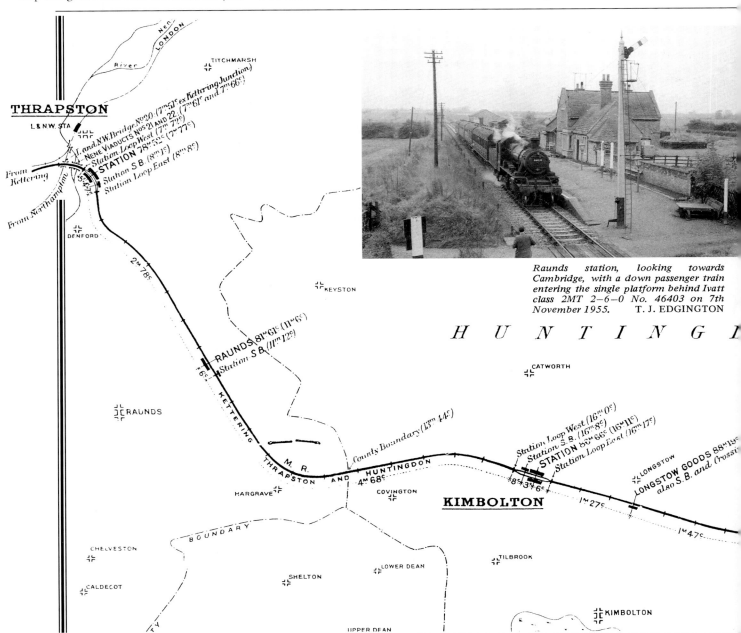

Raunds station, looking towards Cambridge, with a down passenger train entering the single platform behind Ivatt class 2MT 2–6–0 No. 46403 on 7th November 1955.   T. J. EDGINGTON

stock, vehicles, furniture and general merchandise traffic; the crane power was 1 ton 10 cwt.

The Air Ministry sidings at the west end of the station trailed from the up direction. The MR signal cabin, sited to the west of the platforms on the up side, was opened on 29th November 1891 as a replacement for an earlier cabin.

Continuing eastwards from Kimbolton, trains soon reached Longstow goods station (17 miles 44 chains), which provided public goods facilities for coal and other traffic, and also served the needs of a nearby brickworks. A signal box was in operation by the 1880s, and a replacement cabin was brought into use on 11th August 1891. The sidings at Longstow were closed in June 1953.

Still heading eastwards, the line skirted Calper Wood where, at one time, an isolated goods siding had been installed to serve the needs of the Duke of Manchester's estate. Beyond, trains passed another small plantation known as West Wood, after which trains coasted over a level crossing and entered the wayside station at Grafham (20 miles 70 chains).

Grafham was the smallest and arguably the least important stopping place on the line. It consisted of a single platform and goods siding on the down side, the siding being arranged as a loop with connections at each end; the principal sources of traffic handled here were coal and livestock. Grafham's station buildings were constructed of yellow brickwork instead of the local stone that had been used elsewhere on the line from Kettering. The signal cabin, opened on 9th June 1891, was sited to the west of the

Kimbolton station, looking east towards Huntingdon c.1930, with the brick station buildings to the right of the picture.
LENS OF SUTTON

The brick station building at Buckden, photographed from the road overbridge in 1935. The building was essentially an 'L-plan' structure, the booking office wing forming the vertical stroke of the 'L', whilst the cross wing formed the horizontal stroke. An additional half-hipped gable projected from the west end of the house portion.
COLLECTION R. J. ESSERY

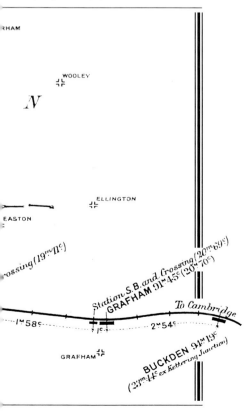

platform on the down side, in convenient proximity to the level crossing.

From Grafham, the route descended steadily through pleasant, though unspectacular rural countryside; a minor road ran more or less parallel to the line on the right-hand side until, after about one mile, it crossed to the north side of the railway by means of an underbridge. To the left meanwhile, the dark outline of Brampton Woods could be glimpsed from the windows of the gently swaying carriages. Passing beneath a minor road bridge, the trains soon passed beneath a more important road overbridge that carried the busy A1 road across the line. Beyond, the route continued eastwards to Buckden, the penultimate stopping place on the Kettering to Huntingdon branch.

Situated some 23 miles 44 chains from Kettering Junction, Buckden had a single platform on the down side of the running line, with a two-siding goods yard immediately to the east; one of the goods sidings formed a loop with trailing connections from each direction, whilst the dead-end siding at the rear of the yard was used for coal and other mileage traffic. The A141 road was carried over the line on an overbridge at the west end of the platform, and there was a standard MR signal cabin on the down side.

Like Grafham, Buckden was provided with a yellow-brick station building. The latter building was an 'L' shaped structure incorporating a two-storey station master's house in the horizontal stroke of the 'L' and a single-storey waiting room wing, the waiting room being parallel to the platform whereas the house portion was at right-angles to the line; the building followed no particular architectural style, its appearance being Victorian domestic rather than Tudor Gothic.

The line continued eastwards beyond Buckden for about a mile, and then curved gradually north-eastwards towards Huntingdon. Crossing the River Ouse on a skew bridge, the Midland route soon passed beneath the Great Northern main line, and, having passed over a small subsidiary channel of the Ouse, ascended a long gradient which brought it up to the level of the East Coast Main Line. At this point the route had originally bifurcated, with one arm continuing northwards into the nearby GNR station while the other diverged north-eastwards towards Godmanchester. Latterly, however, all trains turned north-eastwards onto the GN&GE Joint line, the north-facing spur being abandoned.

Still curving eastwards, the Midland line finally converged with the GN&GE Joint route at the east end of Huntingdon East station (26 miles 13 chains).

As we have seen, this station was opened on 1st May 1883, and although it was sited on GN&GE property it was of typical Great Northern appearance. Three platforms were available, the southernmost platform being an island with tracks on either side. Both sides of the station were covered by flat-topped awnings, and the platforms were linked by a lattice girder footbridge; all three platforms were sharply curved, the station being situated on an east to south curve between the GN&GE and Great Northern lines.

The actual junction between the Midland and GN&GE lines was originally controlled from a standard Great Eastern signal cabin known as Huntingdon East Junction Box, but this was abolished when the junction arrangements were simplified during the 1920s. Thereafter, the station was controlled from the remaining Huntingdon South Junction Box, which was sited at the south end of the station where the GN&GE line joined the Great Northern main line. Midland passenger trains used the outer face of the island platform, there

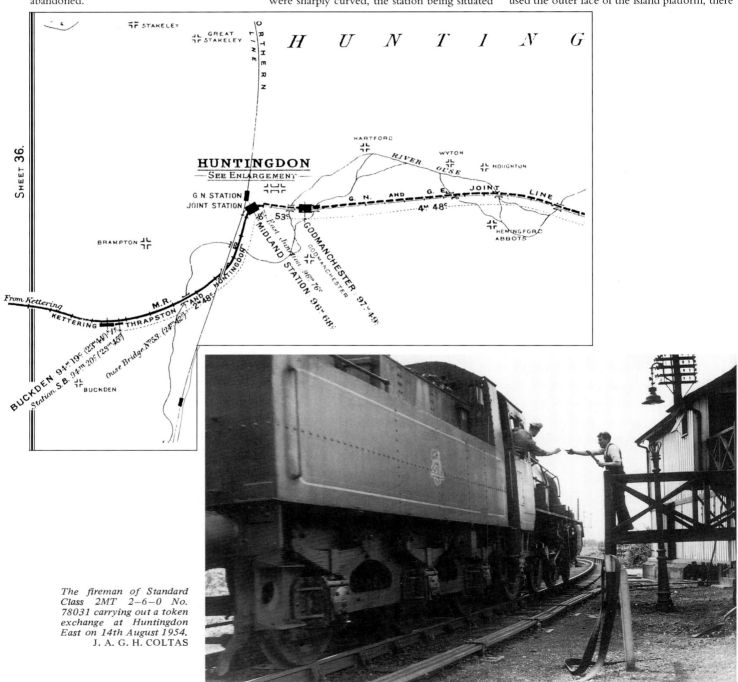

The fireman of Standard Class 2MT 2-6-0 No. 78031 carrying out a token exchange at Huntingdon East on 14th August 1954.
J. A. G. H. COLTAS

being no running connections to or from the two centre tracks.

Other details at Huntingdon East included a small engine shed and turntable at the east end of the station, and five railway cottages to the north. The shed was a single-road, brick-built structure with a gable roof and arched windows on each side; it was erected around 1885 after an earlier shed had been destroyed in an accident. The engine shed siding was flanked by a second locomotive siding which terminated on a small turntable. An open coaling stage stood between the these two engine sidings. The nearby railway cottages were of Great Eastern and Great Northern design, three of these dwellings being of GER appearance whilst the remaining two appeared to be of GNR origin.

There were no goods facilities at Huntingdon East, but ample accommodation was available for freight traffic at Godmanchester, which was only a short distance further east. The latter station was, however, situated on the GN&GE Joint Line and as such it is, strictly speaking, beyond the scope of this present study of the Midland route from Kettering to Huntingdon. Suffice to say, Huntingdon East was never regarded as the eastern terminus of the MR line from Kettering, and branch trains continued for a further twenty miles before reaching their ultimate destination at Cambridge.

THE BRITISH RAILWAYS ERA

The nationalisation of Britain's railway system on 1st January 1948 made little appreciable difference to local routes such as the Kettering to Cambridge line, which continued to operate much as they had done under private ownership. The western section of the Kettering to Cambridge cross-country line inevitably became part of BR's London Midland Region, whilst the eastern end passed into Eastern Region control. The boundary between LMR and ER territory was eventually fixed at the border between Northamptonshire and Huntingdonshire, which meant that around twelve miles of the former Midland line was transferred to the Eastern Region.

In locomotive terms, the Kettering to Cambridge route became something of a joint line; LMS engines had always worked through to Cambridge, but in BR days former Great Eastern classes appeared in increasing numbers on the western section of line between Kettering and Huntingdon.

Tender locomotives continued to predominate, and in 1946 a number of recently-built Ivatt Class 2MT 2–6–0s were allocated to Kettering for use on the line. By 1950, the local allocation included Nos. 46400, 46401, 46402, 46403 and 46494. These engines were later joined by Nos. 46444, 46465, 46466, 46467, 46495 and 46496, one or two examples being allocated to Cambridge shed in order to work services from the eastern end of the route. The Ivatt engines were subsequently joined by BR

Buckden station, looking west towards Kettering on 11th August 1959. The MR signal cabin, which featured small windows at the front and sides, was earlier than the 'Type 2' boxes found elsewhere on the line, although of obvious Midland design. **COLLECTION R. J. ESSERY**

Standard Class 2MT 2–6–0s Nos. 78020 and 78021, both of which were stationed at Kettering in the mid-1950s.

Many of the passenger trains were hauled by former Great Eastern J15 Class 0–6–0s, No. 65390 being a regular performer; this locomotive often worked the first westbound train from Cambridge to Kettering, and then spent the day at Kettering before returning to Cambridge in the late afternoon. Other Worsdell J15 Class 0–6–0s seen on the line during the 1950s included Nos. 654421/65451, 65457, 65474, 65475 and 65477.

Earlier generations of motive power were not entirely absent during the post-war period, and indeed, former Midland 2–4–0 No. 20216 continued to work regularly on the line until it was transferred from Kettering to Gloucester in about 1948.

In addition, the familiar Johnson Class 2F 0–6–0s remained active in the Kettering area for several years. In 1950, for example, Kettering shed housed 2F 0–6–0s Nos. 58162, 58164, 58172, 58183, 58193, 58194, 58195 and 58214. Most of these locomotives appeared on the Kettering to Huntingdon line at one time or another, their usual duties being confined, in the main, to local freight and shunting work.

The line never became a diesel stronghold, and the usual passenger formations continued to be composed of former LMS corridor vehicles. In the early 1950s, these sets were adorned with the then-standard BR carmine and cream livery, but in later years the local trains were repainted in LMS style maroon, which recalled the traditional Midland livery of earlier days.

The train service provided three or four workings each way, with three workings running throughout between Kettering and Cambridge. In 1956, for instance, eastbound workings left Kettering at 8.33 am, 2.09 pm and 5.25 pm, and arrived in Cambridge at 10.20 am, 3.45 pm and 7.22 pm respectively. In the return direction, westbound services left Cambridge at 7.25 am, 11.27 am and 4.55 pm, the arrival times in Kettering being 9.15 am, 1.05 pm and 6.41 pm respectively. There were no Sunday services.

On Saturdays, the line was served by a long-distance through service between Leicester and Clacton, which left Leicester London Road at 8.14 am and Kettering at 9.11 am. Calling intermediately at Thrapston (9.29 am), it continued eastwards via Huntingdon East (10.03 am) and reached Clacton at 1.18 pm. The westbound working left Clacton at 10.50 am and Huntingdon East at 1.49 pm; having called at Thrapston to set-down only at 2.29 pm, the train reached Kettering at 2.58 pm and arrived at Leicester London Road by 3.51 pm.

RUNDOWN AND CLOSURE

Sadly, the later 1950s were a time of decline for rural railways such as the Kettering to Cambridge line. With more and more families having access to a motor vehicle, there was less incentive for people to travel on local railways which were, by any definition, relics of the Victorian era. At the same time, the government of the day was openly hostile towards the now state-owned railway system, and, although vast sums began to pour into road-building schemes, there was no attempt to provide comparable levels of investment for the rail network. In these circumstances, it is hardly surprising that the Kettering to Huntingdon branch should have become a candidate for closure.

In March 1959 it was announced that all passenger services were to be withdrawn between Kettering and Huntingdon. The usual TUCC consultation process was then implemented, two inquiries being necessary because the route spanned two BR regions. Despite numerous objections from individuals and local authorities, the closure decision was confirmed, the overall impression being that the pretended 'consultation' was merely a formality. It was decided that the passenger service would be withdrawn with effect from 15th June 1959, and as that was a Monday, the last trains would be run on Saturday, 13th June 1959.

As happens on such occasions, the final day of operation was an unusually busy day, as numerous people turned up to ride on the doomed railway for the very last time. The final westbound service from Cambridge to Kettering was headed by Ivatt Class 2MT 2–6–0 No. 46496, and it arrived in Kettering at 6.30 pm, driven by driver Frank Maxey and fired by David Freeman. In the opposite direction, the last up train from Kettering to Cambridge left at 8.10 pm behind sister engine No. 46497, with driver Chris Easy and fireman Peter Brown; both trains were composed of four coaches.

The withdrawal of passenger services did not entail complete closure of the line because freight services were retained between Kettering and Kimbolton; Cranford, Thrapstone, Raunds and Kimbolton remained open for public goods traffic, while private siding traffic continued to be handled at the various ironstone sidings along the line. At the eastern end of the route, Huntingdon East station remained open for limited passenger services until September 1959 when it was closed to all traffic; a full passenger service was nevertheless retained on the ex-GER section between Cambridge and St Ives, with trains running on a Cambridge–St. Ives–March axis.

The rundown continued into the 1960s, with the withdrawal of remaining goods services from Cranford in November 1961. In the meantime, the abandoned line eastwards of Kimbolton was lifted, and the former Kettering to Cambridge cross-country route was thereby reduced to separate sections between Kettering and Kimbolton, Huntingdon and Godmanchester, and St Ives to Cambridge. In October 1963, public goods services were withdrawn between Kettering and Kimbolton, and the branch was subsequently cut back to Twywell, where private siding facilities were retained in connection with the still-flourishing iron ore traffic.

Rationalisation of the steel industry gave rise to further changes during the next few years. The surviving blast furnaces in the Kettering and Wellingborough areas ceased production, whilst changes in the steel-making process meant that the local iron ore became unsuitable for the latest production techniques. The local iron ore workings were closed down one by one during the 1960s, but the demise of these traditional industries was made up for, at least to some extent, by the growth of iron concentrate traffic as a by-product of the sand and gravel industry.

A view south-eastwards from the road overbridge at Raunds in May 1960, showing the down starting signal, which featured a Midland post and spike finial, and an upper quadrant arm that had presumably been added during the BR period.
COLLECTION R. J. ESSERY

An Insight into Early Traffic Control

by KEITH MILES

FOLLOWING publication of my experience in one of the advanced postwar control rooms ('Improver Assistant in Control', *Journal* No. 17) I became interested in the earlier arrangements, especially in view of the remark made by David R. Lamb in *Modern Railway Operation* (Pitman, 1941). He said, in relation to the situation prevailing at the outbreak of World War II, 'The London Midland & Scottish possesses the most complete system of train control in Great Britain'. It should be said, nevertheless, that the pre-war system was but an amalgam and subsequent development of those inherited from the constituent companies at grouping. Now, of those companies, only the Midland, London & North Western and Lancashire & Yorkshire could be said to have exercised system-wide supervision, with the Midland being first in the field.

In those days it was usual for the railway companies to accept traffic from customers in whatever quantities and for whatever destinations they cared on a day-to-day basis. In the early 1900s the South Yorkshire and Nottinghamshire coalfields were despatching vast numbers of wagons to meet export orders through the east coast ports as well as for home consumption. The inevitable congestion, apart from anything else, resulted in excessively long hours being worked by train crews. In order to deal with the situation, at the instigation of J.H. Follows, sometime Assistant District Inspector at Normanton but then Traffic Inspector at Derby, an experimental staff control office was established at Masborough. In 1907 there had been more than twenty thousand cases of men working excessively long hours; four years later there were none (*The Midland Railway*, Hamilton Ellis, Malaga Books, 1966).

The evident success of the scheme persuaded the General Superintendent, Cecil Paget, that centralised control of the actual train movements as well would be another step forward. Development of the scheme was entrusted to Follows, who was transferred to the General Superintendent's personal staff for that purpose. The most congested section of the railway, that between Cudworth and Toton, was chosen for the first implementation of the scheme, which came into being in January 1909, with district control offices at Cudworth, Masborough, Staveley, Westhouses and Toton. Not only was the flow of goods and mineral traffic through the section under their supervision, but the acceptance of traffic from the collieries was also regulated. They were no longer allowed to send their wagons of export coal onto the railway until it was known that the designated vessel was ready to receive it, nor was any train of either coal or goods accepted unless a clear path through to its destination could be arranged.

It should be said that none of this would have been possible but for the growth of telephonic communications: indeed, most sources refer to the system as 'telephone control'. The electro-magnetic telephone had been invented by Graham Bell in 1876 and, although there were some 26,000 subscribers in the UK by 1887, it was hardly widespread, and on the railway most communications were by telegraph. However, the Cudworth-Toton pilot traffic control scheme proved to be every bit as successful as the Masborough staff control had been and it was decided to extend the organisation throughout the entire railway, with up to a total of twenty-five district control offices, all responsible to a central control office at Derby.

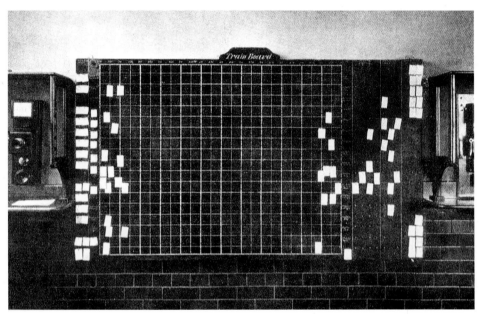

One of Masborough's time-based train control boards, flanked by the circuit telephones by which the operators kept in touch with the various reporting points in the district.

In each district office the movement of trains was registered on two time-based display boards, each portraying twelve hours of the day. The boards were divided both vertically and horizontally, the vertical lines being the time intervals and the horizontal the various signal box reporting points on the district. Each train was represented by a ticket endorsed with particulars of its make-up, motive power and trainmen. On entering the district, the train ticket was pegged on the board at the appropriate time and location and, as it moved through the area, the ticket was moved across the board(s) until it reached its destination or passed into the next district. At either end of the boards were additional columns holding tickets for trains due into the district, traffic waiting to be moved, shunting engines, etc.

While all this was hidden from staff on the ground, very visible features appeared at either end of the trains themselves: engine numbers had been transferred to the tender or tank sides in large, easily discernible numerals and coded train descriptions were displayed in racks on the sides

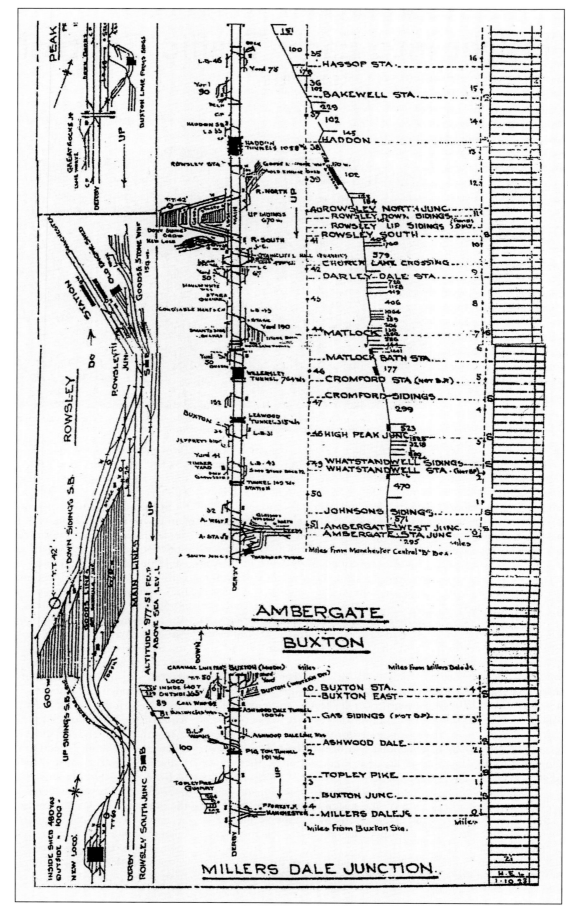

Part of an original side strip diagram for the Rowsley District dated 1923. The enlargement depicts the situation before the new engine shed was actually opened (1926) and the sidings were remodelled (1928/9) to give an increased capacity in the Down Sidings of 845 wagons and 721 in the Up Sidings.

With the side strip diagram in place on the left, a timetabling clerk at work on a 'path diagram' in the Derby Trains Office in 1936. Angled lines depicted trains in motion, horizontal lines trains at rest; whilst full lines represented timetabled paths, dotted lines show unoccupied and thus available paths.
NATIONAL RAILWAY MUSEUM

of the brake vans. Full details of the latter appeared in *Midland Record* No. 2. Follows was also responsible for that long-lasting piece of railway paraphernalia, the 'side strip diagram'. The entire railway system was mapped in the form of line diagrams with selected enlargements of stations, goods yards, etc., each showing all manner of details such as signal boxes, siding capacities, water columns and so on. These were used in conjunction with 'path diagrams', as illustrated in the accompanying photograph, in order to discover the workable capacity of the various sections and to determine the optional paths for the diverse classes of trains, thus to arrive at an organised and effective timetable.

In line with the developments on the Midland, the LNWR established its first centralised control of goods train movements at Springs Branch in September 1912. The obvious efficacy of the arrangement resulted in the expenditure of £36,000 in 1913/14 on the installation of a telephone network for control purposes of all trains other than loaded passenger trains (*The London & North Western Railway*, M.C. Reed, Atlantic, 1996),The system originally extended to thirteen district control offices, mostly reflecting the Midland pattern with time boards, but some, as, for example, Bescot, adopting geographical boards with the trains being pegged in the appropriate positions on the track. The main difference was that the LNW set-up did not include the task of relieving trainmen.

On the Lancashire & Yorkshire Railway a much more sophisticated system had evolved and for a description I'm indebted to Roger Mellor of the L&YR Society and his article 'Central Freight Traffic Control Systems on the L&Y' published in the Spring 2000 edition of their historical journal, *Platform*. As with the other companies, the increasing volume of freight traffic had led to chronic congestion, with the major impediment to an easement being the lack of real time communication. Again, as elsewhere, the perfection of a reliable telephone system suddenly provided a realistic way forward. The first district control offices at

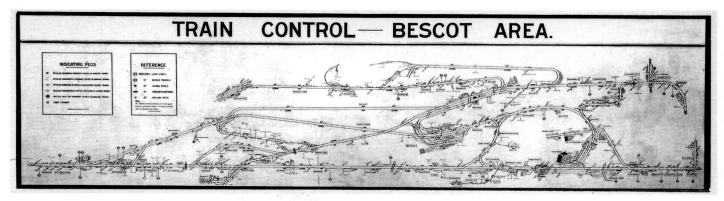

This geographical train control board at Bescot typified the type of arrangement in place at certain LNWR district offices.

Wakefield, Wigan and Liverpool were opened in 1912 with another at Manchester in 1913. A much larger central control office was established at Manchester Victoria in 1915, the controllers from Wakefield and Wigan being transferred over. Nevertheless, the relief of goods guards was retained at the district offices and another was opened at Miles Platting in 1916 for that purpose. Surprisingly, the relief of enginemen was apparently not part of the control function!

The Central Control Office was a large, impressive, circular room, surmounted by a glass dome, situated in the General Superintendent's offices above the New Bridge Street Parcels Office. Within the office, on the whole of the wall above dado level, was a schematic map of the entire L&Y system from Liverpool, Southport and Blackpool in the west to Goole in the east. Below dado level were seventeen Section Controllers' positions, each having a detailed map of the section, giving the wagon capacities of sidings, etc., a dedicated telephone switchboard, a large guard's watch and various holders for forms and train tokens. On an inner raised circle were fourteen positions for the Chief and Deputy Chief Controllers of the Western, Central and Eastern Districts together with those controllers having functional responsibilities such as rolling stock, goods guards, locomotives, etc. On a central raised dais, overseeing all, sat the Master Controller.

Briefly, the signalmen and staff along the route telephoned in the control number by which each train was identified, the engine number, make-up of the train, time of arrival, departure or passing as appropriate. These details were recorded on both a train card and token, the latter pegged on the section board. The act

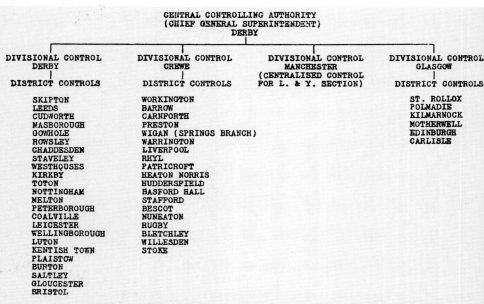

Chart of the LMS control structure soon after grouping, listing all the district and divisional offices.

of inserting the peg completed an electrical circuit that, in turn, illuminated a lamp in the same location on the large schematic map, different colours denoting up or down main-line trains or those in loops and sidings. So, by looking around the room from his central elevated post, the Master Controller could see the position and progress of every freight train on the entire railway.

Of necessity, all the foregoing is but a simplified outline of the three systems with no real mention of some of the ancillary activities such as motive power control and rolling stock control, especially brake vans. Further, it may be noticed that a common factor was the absence of passenger train control at district level. Whilst the movement of passenger trains was recorded, they did not impinge on control arrangements unless something happened out of course. However, from 1923 all three companies were absorbed into the LMS in which J.H. Follows, the architect of the original Midland system, was then the Chief General Superintendent. The MR, LNWR and LYR became the Midland, Western and Central Divisions with the Scottish companies becoming the Northern Division. So far as I'm aware, they had no specific control arrangements whereas, as it happened, the Midland's Scottish partner, the North British, had developed a similar system having an early beginning with a mineral traffic control office at Portobello in 1913. This expanded into a comprehensive organisation based on three centres at Edinburgh, Coatbridge and Burntisland. For the LMS Northern Division, a Midland-style organisation was soon put in place as shown by the accompanying chart.

View from the Master Controller's desk in the Manchester Victoria Central Control Office. The large schematic map covered the wall space with the Section Controllers' positions and detailed maps below. Between them and the Master Controller's position we see the desks of the Chief and Deputy Controllers, etc.

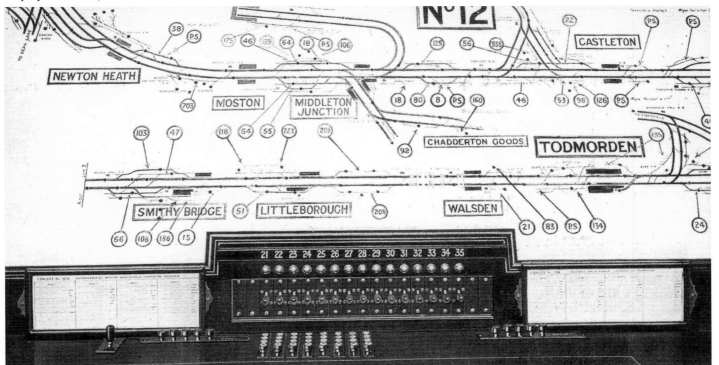

Close-up of Section Controller No. 12's desk with its dedicated detailed map and telephone keyboard.

At the British Empire Exhibition at Wembley in 1925, the LMS promulgated its train control arrangements including full replicas of its passenger control tables at the Derby and Crewe Divisional Offices. These comprised clips, known as 'donkeys' by the Derby people, holding colour-coded cards with train information being moved along rails mounted on the desktop to give a picture of the state of the line. A freely distributed explanatory booklet made the questionable claim that 'even a moment's delay at a signal is known at Derby, Crewe, Manchester or Glasgow almost before the train has restarted'! The working of the less passenger-conscious freight services were also described in more conservative tones: 'By this system of telephonic advice the District Controller knows precisely the location of trains operating on the tracks in his area at any given time, and is able, as required by circumstances, to turn them out of course or otherwise make adjustments as necessitated by traffic conditions.' Coming to the Manchester Victoria Divisional Control Office, however, the writer waxed lyrical: 'The classes of trains are indicated by lights of different colours, and it is a picture reminiscent of fairyland to stand there and watch the lights flitting in and out as the trains pursue their "lawful occasions" through the area.'!

In connection with the latter, R.G. (Dick) Lord, who I later knew as the Assistant District Passenger Manager, Birmingham, in the early 1960s, was appointed as a Grade 4 Relief Clerk at

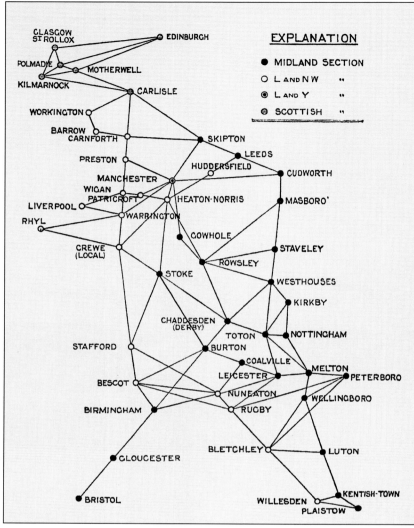

Train control was totally dependent on telephonic communication and this chart, which appeared in the Empire Exhibition booklet, depicted the inter-district network.

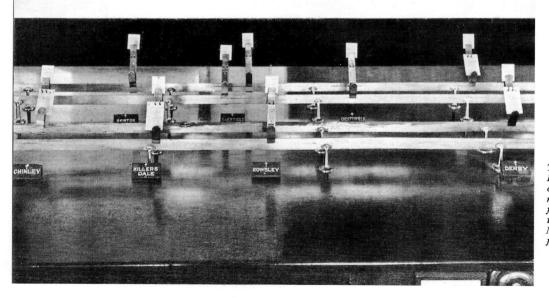

The passenger control table at the Derby Divisional Office with pairs of rails representing the Midland main lines, at 1 inch to the mile, from London to Carlisle, Derby to Birmingham and Derby to Manchester, the latter being in the foreground.

Stalybridge in March 1936 and within his territory was the Yard Master's Office at Miles Platting. This was 'like a sub-control office insofar as the control of goods guards was concerned, including their relief on local freight trains within the area. This relieved the Guards' Controller in the Divisional Control Office of this duty. The clerks had control of a small telephone switchboard and were the contact between all signal boxes and yards in the area – Brewery Sidings, Collyhurst Street, Tank Yard, New Allen Street Coal Yard, Oldham Road, Moston Sidings, Park Station, Park No. 1, Park No. 2, Beswick and the passenger stations at Miles Platting and Park' (*Railways from Grassroots to Management*, Adelphi Press, 1991).

In the Birmingham area, especially at New Street, the former Midland and LNW lines ran cheek by jowl but, despite this close proximity, they still operated as virtually two separate railways. The MR district control room was at Saltley, originally on the station, but moved to a new building near the loco shed in 1937. The LNWR local freight-only district control room had been at Bescot but the predominance of Midland ideas and men in the Operating Department required a change to the Midland pattern with an acknowledgement of passenger services as well. Consequently, a new district control room was set up on the top floor of the office block on New Street's platform 6 in 1925 and the Bescot one closed (*Birmingham New Street – LMS Days*, Richard Foster, Wild Swan, 1997).

Early in 1937, Ernest Lemon, as Vice-President responsible for the Railway Traffic Operating & Commercial Sections, in which post he'd succeeded Follows in late 1931, went with others on an Officers' Tour. During the course of the tour he visited the control offices at Westhouses and Rowsley and found that 'the accommodation was very unsatisfactory and the staff had to work under considerable difficulties'. As a result, 'a review of the layout and equipment of control offices was speedily ordered, and it was further decided that an ideal "theoretical" control should be built with a miniature geographical board, incorporating all of what was then the latest ideas in respect of cabinets and telephones' (*London Midland & Scottish – a Railway in Retrospect*, Hamilton Ellis, Ian Allan, 1970). The chosen site for the 'theoretical' control was in No. 19,

Rowsley District Control Office in 1942 with Arnold Kingman seated at the far end of the table. Opened in 1912, it was first sited at the station but was later moved to a purpose-made building at the south end of the up sidings. ROWSLEY ASSOCIATION COLLECTION

One lasting feature of the control arrangements made in the Northern Division was that the target boards carried on the shunting/trip engines had the number preceded by the initial letter of the control district in which the job worked or originated. The practice continued into BR days and here in 1954 at Greenock, Princes Pier, 47169 was carrying target P251.
CTY. REX CONWAY

The 1941 replacement control room at Birmingham New Street with three section controllers at the train board and the guards, motive power and passenger controllers at the curved range of desks.

Euston Square, one of a terrace of houses on the north side facing Friends House.

The layout had many advantages over the existing arrangements: hand microphones fitted above desk level, all telephone cables concealed, all lamp signals directly associated with the circuit telephone, an engaged lamp signal given throughout the office on any circuit that was in use, thus preventing a member of the office interrupting a colleague, duplicate independent telephones provided, one on each side of the desk for the omnibus circuits, all telephones wired in parallel to avoid complete failure through a fault on any one of them and all illuminated by indirect lighting. Subject to some minor alterations, the equipment was adjudged to be suitable for the improvement of the Company's control offices. The first to be so treated was that at Wellingborough, using, as it happened, part of the equipment from Euston Square. Then followed Kirkby and Westhouse, but the outbreak of war put a stop to further progress.

When the impending hostilities became imminent, thoughts turned to the operation of the control system in the event of aerial attack. It was decided to construct air-raid shelters adjacent to the control offices, complete with almost duplicate facilities to allow the control function to continue during raids. Local conditions varied the design to some extent, but what might be called the 'standard' control shelter had an entrance air lock, control room and three other small rooms housing a telephone switchboard, batteries and generator. The basic structure consisted of two concrete walls, one 3ft thick, the other 1ft 6in, separated by a 4ft sand-filled cavity. The roof was of similar construction, two layers of reinforced concrete, one 4ft thick, the other 2ft, again separated by a 4ft sand-filled void. The whole was supposed to withstand a direct hit from bombs of up to 500lbs in weight.

That at Birmingham New Street required design modifications since it was built under platform 1A to the west of the Navigation Street bridge. It was in use on 16th October 1940 when No. 5 signal box was almost totally destroyed by the blast from a bomb that fell nearby, and again twelve days later when a firebomb hit the platform 6 office block and rendered the control office unusable. The staff were condemned to suffer the cramped and claustrophobic shelter accommodation until a rebuilt permanent office became available one year later. Surprisingly, this was built in the same location as before but was now in the updated style of the Euston 'theoretical' design.

I'm not aware of the location of the shelter for the Divisional Control Room staff at Manchester Victoria but one must have been provided, especially in view of the disastrous events of December 1940. There is evidence, however, that other staff were not so securely protected. Dick Lord was working in the Booking Office at the time and 'when the sirens sounded, all cash was gathered together and the whole staff trooped down to the air raid shelter which was the cellar underneath Hunts Bank. I'm afraid it would not have offered much protection if bombs had dropped since one could hear the ponies with the *Evening Chronicle* vehicles trotting on the roadway above which was, in fact, the roof of the cellar.' He goes on to record that on the night of 23rd/24th 'a bomb had dropped close to platform 17, demolishing the Guards' Room and the Divisional Control Room which was completely destroyed together with the master train diagram. The whole organisation for the train planning and control of the running of the trains had broken down.' Up to the time of writing, I have been unable to ascertain, despite numerous enquiries, what measures were taken to restore order. Was the original control room rebuilt or was it replaced by one of the Euston-style layouts?

The shelter with which I was most familiar was at Willesden Junction, on the opposite side of the station approach from the control office on the first floor of the platform 9 buildings. This, by the way, was one of the LNW offices with a geographical board as evidenced by the 'Behind the Scenes' article in a January 1938 issue of *The Willesden Chronicle*: 'The Control Office was established in 1913. By means of a large plan in front of the operators upon which the lines are mapped and moveable indicators are placed, the operators can see at a glance where and how trains are moving and by telephone can intimate to each section how, when and where those movements can be regulated with best results.' As with the ARP design signal boxes, the postwar difficulty with the shelters was the problem of their demolition (see 'A New Broom', *Journal* No. 8). The concrete blockhouse of the Willesden example remained in situ and proved to be an obstacle to the development of staff accommodation on the adjacent land in the 1970s. I've been led to believe that the local authority acquired it for use as a nuclear bunker!

The postwar years saw the deferred implementation of a modernised control structure with fewer, larger district offices. Gone were the white-on-black display boards similar to the signal box diagrams of the day, replaced by a green-based board with the lines in different colours to indicate main, goods, loops and sidings, etc.

And here's a puzzle: I have in my possession a copy of a white-on-black board depicting Rowsley District Control but I'm assured by Arnold Kingman, the sole remaining member of staff from that office, that it was never installed in its intended location. Can it be that, in view of Lemon's visit in 1937, this was the board in his 'theoretical' control room?

Willesden Junction in October 1980, with the former LNWR district control office on the first floor of the buildings on the left (now the Area Manager's Office) and the wartime air-raid shelter on the right.
J. C. GILHAM

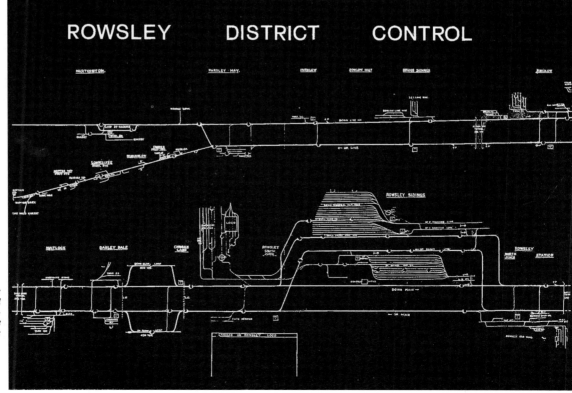

The centre portion of the Rowsley District Control black-on-white geographical train board. The holes for the train card pegs are clearly visible.

This picture was taken at Muir of Ord on 21st May 1928, where the line from Fortrose joined the main line from Inverness to Wick and Thurso. The rather elderly-looking locomotive was a Highland Sky Bogie, now running as LMS No. 14277. One source has stated that because the Sky Bogies were regarded as 'mixed traffic' locomotives, they were not named. This example was built in 1882 and withdrawn in June 1930. H. C. CASSERLEY

THE SCOTTISH LOCAL COMMITTEE
by L. G. WARBURTON

THE editor requested me to provide information on the LMS Scottish Local Committee with regard to its formation, composition and responsibilities. The following is correct for the initial couple of years following the grouping in 1923.

The first LMS Board meeting was informal and held at Euston Station on 15th December 1922, with the LNWR Minute Book used to record the proceedings, with the minutes for the new company starting at number one.

THE SCOTTISH LOCAL COMMITTEE

Item 6 on the agenda was the setting up of the Scottish Local Committee for the management of the railways in the Scottish Division, which consisted of four Directors from the Board of the Company, one of which was the Chairman, and ten other members (such number being subject to reduction from time to time at the Board's discretion) who 'are not Directors of the Company, but are Proprietors domiciled in Scotland and holding not less than £2500 of stock in the Company, or such other qualification as may be decided by the Board from time to time, to be co-opted under Section 3 (1) (c) of the Railways Act 1921, and that Mr C. Kerr of the GSWR and Mr Albert E. Pullar of the HR be nominated thereon as two of the four representatives of the Board of the LMSR.' No remuneration was payable to Directorial members of the Committee but non-Directorial members were each to receive £600 per annum. The Committee was to meet in Glasgow and a clerk appointed, coming under the jurisdiction of the Company Secretary. Two members were to meet weekly for the purpose of certifying accounts, including salaries and wages.

Work in the Scottish Division was to be performed by Divisional Officers directly responsible to the Deputy General Manager (for Scotland), and for departmental matters, to the several Chief Officers of the Company, subject to the overriding control of the General Manager of the Company. The Scottish Committee were to meet in the week preceding the week in which the Board in London sat,

To me the Sky Bogies were very 'Highland', so no apologies are offered for including this view of No. 14279 shunting at Kyle of Lochalsh on 20th June 1927. Built in 1893, this locomotive was withdrawn in October 1927. Although I cannot identify all the carriages on the platform line, two were ex-Midland vehicles, further examples of transferring stock from England to replace time-expired HR coaching stock.   H. C. CASSERLEY

to give time to submit recommendations and decisions to be ratified by the Board. A report was also to be prepared for the Board dealing with the principal features of the previous month's working which was to include traffic receipts, hotels and catering, steamers, receipts and expenses and capital expenditure.

The Scottish Committee could authorise work costing up to £500, but any staff appointment with a salary exceeding £350 required Board approval. The general policy and applications for Parliamentary Powers could only be dealt with by the Board and any litigation in the High Courts also required Board approval.

The first official Board Meeting was attended by all Directors except Sir John Field Beale, KBE (ex-MR), and took place on 5th January 1923 when all the appointments made to date were ratified with the Scottish Local Committee appointed as follows in Minute 40.

Caledonian
Messrs. Henry Allan; William Younger; James Hamilton Houldsworth; Henry Erskin Gordon, CBE; Frederick Bower Sharp and James Whiteford Murray.

Glasgow and South Western
Messrs. Charles Kerr, CA; Sir Alexander Gracie, KBE, MVO; Sir James Bell, Bart. and David Cooper.

Highland
Messrs. Albert E. Pullar; Sir Hector Munro, Bart. and Robert W. Wilson.

At the Board Meeting on 2nd March 1923 (minute 93), Henry Allan (ex-CR) was appointed Chairman with Charles Kerr (ex-GSWR) as Deputy Chairman; J. J. Haining was appointed Secretary and Treasurer. Sir James Bell (ex-GSWR) had declined membership of the Committee.

The resignation of the Chairman Henry Allan was reported at the Board meeting on 27th July (minute 339), with Mr C. Kerr (ex-GSWR) appointed as the new Chairman with Mr. W. Younger (ex-CR) as Deputy Chairman.

REORGANISATION OF COMMITTEES, SCOTTISH ORGANISATION

The Board meeting on 30th November, minute 443, recorded that minute 358 had called for a small committee to report on the future organisation of Committees, etc, whose recommendations were presented including the allocation of the Scottish Directors to the various committees. There were 27 Directors, but as the Chairman and Deputy Chairmen were ex-officio members of all Committees, 24 Directors were available for allocation.

The current arrangement was that meetings were spread over Wednesdays and Thursdays of each Board meeting week, and it was recommended that the main committees met on the Wednesday of each Board week, which were Land & Rating, Works, Law & Medical, Hotels & Catering, Traffic, Shipping, Rolling Stock and Stores. This left the Finance, General Purposes, Special and Sub-Committees to meet on the Thursday. It was also agreed that no Director should sit on more than three Committees and that the Board Chairman should make the appointments and the Chairman of each Committee should decide on which Company Officers he desired to attend his meeting.

A separate Secretary was to be appointed by the General Manager for each Committee, with the Secretary of the Company acting as Secretary to the Finance and General Purposes Committees. It was also considered desirable for Directors from time to time to change Committees in order for each Director 'to keep himself conversant with the whole business of the company through the work of the different Committees'. In particular it was considered desirable for the Rolling Stock, Shipping and Works, etc, Committees to occasionally meet at different centres.

As far as the Scottish Organisation was concerned, Messrs Kerr and Pullar had pointed out defects in the current arrangements, suggesting that two members of the Board attended meetings of the Scottish Committee, which was agreed as well as having the Scottish Directors on the Euston Committees.

As might be expected in such a large organisation, the initial delegation of departmental arrangements, would, in the light of experience, require fine-tuning, and the General Manager made the following recommendations at the Board meeting on 25th January 1924, minute 515: that Mr Ramsden and Sir Edwin Stockton become the Company's English representatives on the Scottish Local Committee. The Board meeting on 27th March granted them fees of £200 each per annum for membership of this Committee (minute 595).

The Deputy Chairman, Mr. W. Younger, resigned (minute 535) as had J. G. Stewart on 18th February 1924 (minute 555) and were replaced by Lt. Col. Sir Hugh Arthur Rose of Messrs. Craig & Rees, Ltd of Leith, and Lt. Col. The Hon. James Younger, DSO, of Messrs. George Younger & Son, Ltd, Alloa, and this was agreed at the Board meeting on 1st May 1924 (minute 653).

H. E. Gordon resigned on 21st October 1924 (minute 868) and Major Ralph Glynn G.C. was nominated for the vacancy (minute 985) at the 18th December 1924 meeting.

This undated view was taken at Wick. The Highland owned a number of small 'four coupled' tank engines and whilst the identity of this locomotive is not known, I can say it is one of the series that became LMS 15051-15054, which were built in 1905 and three remained in service at Nationalisation. The two leading vehicles in the train were elderly Highland stock, but the coach at the end of the train was an ex-Midland carriage, one of several that were transferred to Scotland after the grouping.
COLLECTION R. J. ESSERY

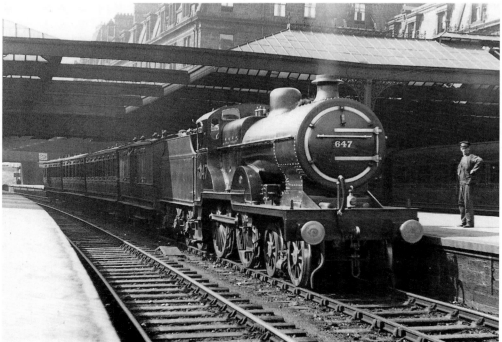

For the next picture, we move to the Glasgow & South Western Railway at Ayr and show a new LMS Standard Class 2P 4–4–0 No. 647 with a train of elderly carriage stock. The note on the reverse of the print states 'on a northbound passenger'. However, the locomotive headcode was not correct for a passenger train, so perhaps the fireman had not set the headcode!
COLLECTION R. J. ESSERY

A year after this picture was taken in 1926, the Royal Scots were coming into service, but in many respects it could be argued that this picture was more typical of the LMS than the Royal Scots! Although the focus of attention for the majority of enthusiasts was on the main lines, to many who used the railway on a regular basis the branch and secondary lines provided their experience of the railway system. This picture shows an Ordinary passenger train made up of elderly oil-lit six-wheel carriages hauled by ex-G&SWR 0-4-2 No. 261 running as LMS 17065. The locomotive was a renewal of a James Stirling '221' Class and this example was renewed in 1902 and remained in service until withdrawn in November 1928.
COLLECTION R. J. ESSERY

Overleaf: *As many readers will know, I was born in Birmingham, which helps to explain why, over the years, both LMS Journal and Midland Record have included a number of articles about the area. For the past few months, almost all my time has been devoted towards the preparation of a book about the railways in the greater Birmingham area. The illustrations are the work of one man, the late D. J. Norton, whose pictures have been made available to me by his son, Mark Norton. Regular readers will recall the lead article in the LMS Journal 85th Anniversary Edition about Wolverhampton, a largely photographic feature using D. J. Norton's pictures, so you will have some idea of what this new work will be like. We plan to launch it at the Warley Model Railway Club National Exhibition to be held at the NEC Birmingham on 22nd/23rd November. To provide readers with a taste of New Street station, which figures in the work, we have included this picture which was taken around the time when D. J. Norton began to record the railway scene in the area. This shows the Western Division side of the station, taken from Platform 6, looking towards the rear of the Queen's Hotel, which backed onto the station. The footbridge enabled pedestrians to walk across the station area from the station approach at Stephenson Street to Station Street on the other side of the station. Note No. 3 signal box mounted over the footbridge with the large clock above. Following the end of the Second World War, the roof over the Western side was removed and when this picture was taken in 1946, work had begun. Within a few years, this side of the station totally changed and later the entire station was rebuilt, but that is another story.*

Continued from page 50

Many rare and interesting locomotives have passed through Bromsgrove and the Lickey Incline over the years. One most notable event was a special train hauled by two ex-GWR 'Saint' class 4—6—0s in September 1950. Being 2920 *Saint David* and 2937 *Clevedon Court*, both were amongst the last remaining types and were from Hereford shed. An illustration in a contemporary issue of *Trains Illustrated* shows the pair making the ascent with 58100 on the rear.

John S. Dales
Cofton Hackett, Worcs.

Reading John Edgington's review of the late David Jenkinson's book *Highland in LMS Days* in *LMS Journal 21*, reminded me of an LMS Board minute made on 26th March 1925 in praise of the new LMS regime. One cannot help but contemplate on this letter, and maybe we, as railway enthusiasts, tend to view our favourite line through rose-tinted glasses, when in reality things were not quite so good as we thought they were!

L. G. Warburton

Minute 1093
Railway facilities at Wick
The Chairman submitted a communication which had been addressed by Mr. G. A. O. Green, the Provost of Wick, to the Minister of Transport, (Appendix 'B') from whom it had been received, expressing great appreciation of the improvement in the railway facilities at Wick.

Appendix 'B'

Wick
14th March, 1925

The Rt. Hon. E. Cunliff Lister,
H.M. President Board of Trade,
London.

Sir,

London Midland & Scottish Railway

May I, as the Provost of the Capital of the County of Caithness and the largest town North of Inverness, venture to express my profound gratitude, on behalf of this Northern community, for the great advantages which have accrued to all communities in the North of Scotland in the grouping of the Highland Railway with the London Midland & Scottish Railway?

I may frankly state that, under the old Highland railway, I, as a member of the Wick Town Council and a Magistrate of this town, was one of that Railway Company's severest critics for what I considered was their neglect of the public interest and lack of public facilities, and the entire absence of a progressive spirit in the conduct of the railway.

Now, under the grouping system, the scene has been entirely changed and the Northern communities are enjoying benefits undreamt of some years ago. These benefits I now desire to acknowledge with profound gratitude. The benefits accruing to the whole public of the North of Scotland may be succinctly stated thus:-

1. The rolling stock is of the most modern description and provide the very latest comforts for the travelling public.
2. Dining cars are conveniently run on the two daily trains from Inverness, and travellers have thus all possible facilities and comfort, converting a journey from Inverness, which was formerly looked upon as a nightmare, into what several travellers have expressed to me is now a luxury.
3. The atmosphere of management of this Railway has also undergone a complete change. Now we have a management evincing the greatest interest in the public comfort, anxious to receive and welcome suggestions for the improvement of the railway service, and gladly appreciating every suggestion for the improvement of the system, always keeping in view the avoidance of an unnecessary burden or expense upon the system.
4. This helpful and congenial atmosphere is obvious from the highest to the lowest servant of the Company, and altogether it is obvious that there has been a welcome infusion of life blood of progress, efficiency and energy into the whole service, reflecting the very greatest credit upon the management and the greatest advantage to the general public.
5. Under the old regime, we in Wick, at the terminus of the system, got accustomed to the trains running continually late. Indeed, we ultimately came to accept a train being an hour or so late as being quite in time. Now it is a most unusual concurrence to find a train even a few minutes late at any time.

I hold no brief for any particular official of the management, and have no ulterior object whatever, except the public interest, in writing you thus, but I feel I would be lacking in my duty to the public and to the managers of the LMS Railway in the North of Scotland if I did not express my grateful thanks for, and public acknowledgment of, the tremendous improvement which has been effected to communities in the North of Scotland by the grouping of the Railway system.

I am Sir,
Your obedient Servant,
(Sgd) G. A. O. Green
Provost of Wick

Cover picture — The date is after 1928, the engine number is on the side of the cab but before January 1935. No shed plate on the smokebox door.

Page 1 caption — Yes, the North pilot always stood there.

Page 8 — 82 was not the train reporting number. [W82 was the 1/55 Wolverhampton—Euston. 82 was the Oxenholme target number. Agreed it is a target number but why was it being displayed? We reproduced the caption written by the late E. D. Bruton. Can any reader comment further?] As the train started from Manchester Victoria/Liverpool Exchange it would have carried a Central Division reporting number (CXXX).

Page 48 — I am sure the ticket has not been used. The clips are too neat. Cancellations? Furthermore, the ticket is not dated nor had any of the coupons been collected.

Page 62 — The train engine was ailing and the driver requested a fresh engine at Birmingham New Street and an additional banker at Bromsgrove.

John Edgington
York

Further information

In many respects the three volumes of *Historical Locomotive Monographs* were the precursors to the *LMS Locomotive Profile* series, so it seems appropriate to include all additional information under a single heading. I was delighted to receive this letter from Bob Dearnning, which is reproduced below, but what were LNWR 'Super Ds' doing that far west? I was familiar with them at Washwood Heath when they arrived from the Walsall line, but to work further west seems unusual. Does any reader have any further information?
Editor

Because of an ankle injury, I was unable to walk very far during May/June this year, so I went through my library to re-read some of the more interesting titles. Amongst others, *LMS & LNER Garratts* by Essery and Toms. On pages 58/59, photographs by W. Potter show a Garratt at Gloucester in 1952 with a query 'did they ever work through to Bristol?'.

The answer is yes. I well remember seeing a Garratt on Barrow Road shed during 1951 or 1952, and often kick my own rear for not taking the trouble to photograph the loco. It was stabled on a back road that contained three small turntables used to get 1 to 4F and 1 & 2P locos into the shop that ran as a CMEE outpost on piecework at Derby prices!

I then tried to confirm my sighting, difficult now because few ex-Barrow Road staff are still with us. I eventually was referred to a local railway society, based in Mangotsfield, who turned up trumps and sent me details of sightings west of Gloucester. With their permission, I attach a copy for you and consider that the 9/11/51 or 26/6/52 was my most likely sighting.

Hope this may help you in filling a small gap in information.

Bob Dearnning
Downend, South Glos.

Copy from Mangotsfield Railway Society

Beyer Garratts at Bristol
47978 Saturday, 24/2/51, on Barrow Road at 2/50
47987 Monday, 26/2/51, at Bristol
47997 + 1 other Friday, 9/11/51, freights into Westerleigh Yard
47975 Saturday, 21/6/52, on Barrow Road (on Barnwood 22/6/52)

'Duck Eights' at Bristol
49425 Sunday 29/3/51, on Barrow Road
49395 Thursday, 24/5/51 at Bristol
49432 July 1959, photographed at Barrow Road